The Process Manager

Third edition

"A system is a network of interdependent components that work together to try to accomplish the aim of the system."

W Edwards Deming, *The New Economics for Industry, Government, Education*, MIT Press 1993

"Leadership implies working on the system to continually improve it, with the help of the people."

Myron Tribus

D1232221

Process Management International

Transforming goals into results

Villiers Court • Birmingham Road

Meriden Business Park

Meriden • CV5 9RN • UK

Tel: +44 (0)1676 522766

E-mail: info@pmi.co.uk • Website: www.pmi.co.uk

Thanks to those who have contributed to and developed the material used in this booklet.

Published by
Process Management International Ltd

First edition published 2000 (0-9540605-0-4)
Second (revised) edition published 2004
Reprinted 2006
Third (revised) edition published 2009

ISBN
978-0-9540605-2-7

Table of Contents

Introduction

In 1984 we called our company Process Management International, in response to the growing quality improvement movement.
Back then the word 'process' was associated with continuous manufacture of chemicals, for example, or perhaps with computers. We saw that all work is a process, and that managing and improving processes would be everyone's job.

Almost everyone now recognises the significance of process understanding as the basis of any job, in every organisation, anywhere in the world. At PMI we have validated this idea thousands of times across the world.

Therefore, this handbook is for everyone who wants to ensure that their responsibilities produce the outputs that they should, in an efficient and flexible manner. In addition, the circumstances surrounding their jobs are constantly changing, leading to a sometimes disconcerting need to match consistency with improvement.

There is much jargon associated with quality and improvement, arising out of its long history since the 1920s.

The key common denominators of the approaches, no matter what their name, are:
- system and process management,
- optimisation.

Every manager will, in future, need to understand their business processes, their place in the system, and be able to monitor and improve them in real time, to get them on target with minimum variation.

This handbook summarises the basic methods to do this analysis and improvement work. Any manager who can use this tool set in a wide variety of circumstances, in a cooperative manner with teams at any level in the organisation, is well on the way to thriving in any environment. There are many other, more complex tools: our experience is that those who understand this basic set first can most easily decide which of the more sophisticated ones are useful when they really need them.

The common root of business improvement: The teachings of Dr W Edwards Deming

There have been many contributions to this revolution in thinking, but W Edwards Deming (1900-93) provided a universal framework and foundation for changes that can lead to major operational benefits. The sustained application of these theories and management philosophy lies at the heart of PMI's success with its clients.

Deming summarised his approach into a four-part system for learning, calling it a System of Profound Knowledge. The profound aspect comes from developing and understanding of all four elements, integrating them into everyday thinking, and seeing the extraordinary impact this can have on processes and people, and hence on results.

This model helps us to understand:
1. The interconnected, interdependent nature of our systems and processes.
2. The degree of diversity in all its components and how they vary in their interactions.
3. The continual changes that are taking place and the scope for learning about them, and leading change constructively.
4. The human aspects of engagement, motivation and commitment to the improvement and leadership efforts.

"You get what you get by thinking what you think."

In all of PMI's work we emphasise the
need for challenging one's assumptions,
and developing new thinking, whilst
recognising the need of practical
methods to improve results quickly.

The problem is that much thinking is
unconscious and thus hard to change.
In using the methods in this book,
you should integrate their practical
application with the rethinking of your
assumptions and reactions to work.

Thinking about the system of profound knowledge

There is no need to become an expert in all or any of the four parts of
the System of Profound Knowledge, but it is essential to become aware
of all and their interconnections. This book uses the structure System
of Profound Knowledge as chapters. It –

1. helps readers understand their processes and projects, and relate
   them to customers and suppliers–the whole system;
2. is concerned with representing the data in and around the
   process, and making sense of the variation;
3. is about learning itself, and provides the basis for defining process
   and project purpose, at both general and specific levels, so as to
   establish the target from which variation can be measured;
4. touches upon the complex issues of getting the team together,
   bringing all its talents to bear, and reviewing progress in a
   disciplined manner.

The book is designed as a backup to those who have experienced
PMI's formal learning processes, led either by PMI themselves, their
authorised presenters, or e-Learning platforms. As their learning
process progresses through training, application and discussion, many
readers develop new insights into the wider world through the structure
offered by the System of Profound Knowledge.

The organisation as a system

All systems, both natural and human, are interconnected in some way. Defining the organisation as a system is a first step to understanding the big picture.

"A system is a network of interdependent components that work together to try to accomplish the aim of the system."

W. Edwards Deming, *The New Economics*, MIT Press 1993

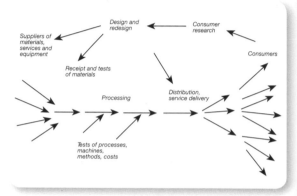

Deming first used a version of this system model in 1950, including customers and suppliers, and the flow of materials and information. We apply it with management teams, helping them to understand the whole organisation; the first step to optimising it.

Major system components

An organisational system can be summarised as three major parts or subsystems, focusing on the "Gemba" or core processes.

- The 'Gemba' are those parts of the system which add value to inputs in the customers' interests. Leaders and workers in Gemba processes can measure their success in external customer focused terms.
- Support processes enable the Gemba to operate. Their success is measured by how well they enable the Gemba to function effectively.
- Strategic and change processes take feedback from customers to the organisation itself and the environment in order to develop policies and lead major changes to the Gemba and support processes.

Learning how to do it

The methods in this handbook work when they are applied diligently,
and this requires confident leadership. In our experience there is
absolutely no substitute for practical experience in using the methods
if one wishes to be able to lead their use. No-one we have met who
has only read books, watched videos or listened to presentations, has
appreciated both the potential they offer and the barriers that restrain
them. We strongly recommend all readers to ensure that they practise
on their own processes, with help from experienced facilitators.
This will build their confidence, only then will they have the basis for
ensuring they are applied to the critical business issues.

Adopting this approach

"Survival is not compulsory"
W Edwards Deming

The ability to improve performance, both for products and services, is crucial to the health of businesses, industries and the larger economy.

Even for seemingly successful businesses, focusing their improvement efforts on fixing problems to maintain the status quo, will not allow them to stay successful in the future.

Today, they must focus their efforts on managing, improving and re-inventing their business processes to continually optimise their business systems.

All organisations must reduce the impacts of their operations on the environment. Whether this is by direct reduction of waste or in changing travel patterns, the first step is to understand how their system works and improving or changing the processes in it.

In summary, Systems Thinking and Process Management:

1. Provide the focus for developing common aims for the organisation.
2. Lead to consistancy of language for work, management, and improvement across the whole organisation.
3. Emphasise the connections between system components, and simulate communication and teamwork.
4. Demand the consideration and understanding of customer and supplier issues, and the recognition of these 'outsiders' as part of an organisation's system. The benefits of cooperation become tangible.
5. Support the effective introduction of new information technology and other technological solutions.
6. Allow and encourage the sensible prioritisation of improvement efforts within the context of the whole.
7. Demand the understanding and reduction of variation in process measures, improving the ability to assess the capability of the process and the likely conformance of the outputs.
8. Encourage widespread and continued learning. This in turn leads to a more knowledgeable, versatile and flexible workforce that, over time, will make an increasing contribution to the organisation's success

Requirements of a Process Manager

Bringing these system ideas together changes the definition of a leader.

"Everyone works in a system.
Leadership involves working on the system,
to continually improve it.
Everyone helps."
Myron Tribus

How do I do that?

1. Understand your place in the organisation.
2. Understand your process.
3. Understand process management.
4. Understand how to lead step change improvement.

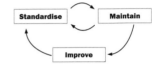

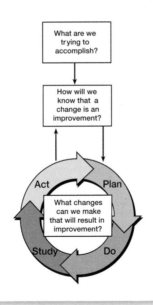

Structure of PMI's teaching in process management and improvement

PMI has developed an integrated series of development and training processes. They apply to all staff from directors to shop floor, with a particular emphasis on change agents and trainers.

Improvement Cycle

Used by Project Leaders in managing step changes in the processes

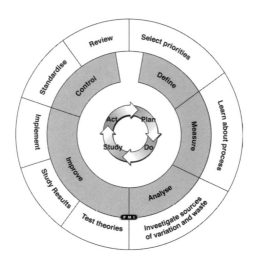

Process Management Cycle

Used by those involved in managing processes day to day

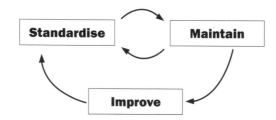

Systems and processes

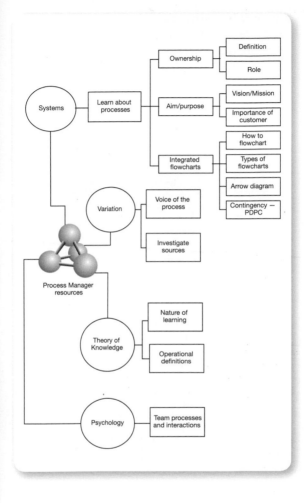

Learning about processes

All work is a process

"A system is a network of interdependent components that work together to try to accomplish the aim of the system."

W Edwards Deming, The New Economics, MIT Press 1993

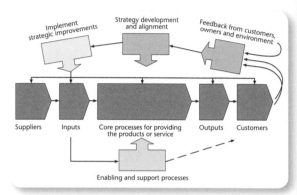

Understanding the implications of this model can provide the basis of planning for the transformed organisation.

- The system includes customers and suppliers.
- The organisation requires an aim, which needs to be understood and shared by those within it.
- Sub-processes need to be managed and improved with the intention of optimising the **whole** system.

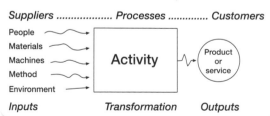

Process improvement involves:

- understanding the process and its aims;
- understanding the variation(s) within the process and its inputs;
- working to reduce variation, then to align the mean with the intended aim.

A strategy for process improvement

Success in managing and improving processes comes with seeing it as the way things are done, rather than regarding it as a set of special tools to be brought into use for particular problems. This requires much dialogue and reflection in its development. However, if you follow this simple strategy you will ensure that all actions are more productive and less likely to conflict with other parts of the organisation.

```
┌─────────────────────────┐
│  Select a process for   │
│       improvement       │
└─────────────────────────┘
            │
            ▼
┌─────────────────────────┐
│      Learn about        │
│      the process        │
│  • Purpose?             │
│  • Customers and their  │
│    requirements?        │
│  • Flow?                │
│  • Collect and study    │
│    data?                │
│  • Ownership?           │
│  • Suppliers and        │
│    capabilities?        │
│  • Problems in the      │
│    process?             │
└─────────────────────────┘
            │
            ▼
┌─────────────────────────┐
│  Select an opportunity  │
│     for improvement     │
└─────────────────────────┘
            │
            ▼
┌─────────────────────────┐
│   Improve the process   │
│  • Process stability    │
│  • Improve process      │
│    capability           │
└─────────────────────────┘
```

Process definition

A series of related steps to understand how the work is done, who for, who is responsible for its design and development, for its execution, and who supplies essential inputs.

Flowcharts

A flowchart outlines a clear, agreed definition of a process.

Benefits

Flowcharts:

- Help build a shared picture of the process, clarifying what needs to be done and by whom.
- Uncover duplication of effort, delays, omissions and unnecessary steps.
- Compare the actual with the ideal process.
- Clarify relationships with other parts of the organisation.
- Explain the process to new employees and others.

Flowcharts may be used –

- at different stages of the strategy for process improvement, from Study to Planning;
- to answer different questions, depending upon the level of detail and information required;
- to provide the basis for BS-EN-ISO 9000 documentation.

Flowcharting should start at the highest appropriate level so that the team can see the big picture and it –

- explores detail as it becomes more focused;
- avoids diving into the wrong part of the process. It also enables backtracking and making mid-course corrections in recognising priorities for improvement;
- can see how changes in one part of a process might affect other parts or processes.

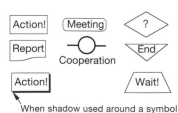

When shadow used around a symbol it indicates that further detail can be found in another chart.

Tips for flowchart construction

Always consider what you are trying to accomplish before constructing the chart. Decide which is the most appropriate chart and the necessary information to include in the chart. For example, if the flow of the process passes from one organisational unit to another, consider an integrated flowchart. (See page 1-6.)

For clarity on all types of flowcharts:

- Label them to identify the process, the activity, author, and date.
- Use defined symbols to depict the steps or events.
- Be sure that the time sequence of the key steps/events follows from top to bottom.
- Use only one connecting line from each box, unless showing a decision or cooperation.
- If possible, the direction of the arrows for Yes/No decisions should be consistent.
- Use only vertical and horizontal lines.
- Keep flowcharts to 6-12 steps, certainly no more than 15.
    - If they exceed 15, they are probably too detailed; an additional chart at a lower level should be considered.
- Start with a broad perspective.
- It is often helpful to include a column on the right side of the chart for comments.
- **Keep it simple!**

Linear flowcharts are the simplest form. They are used to provide a picture of overall flow

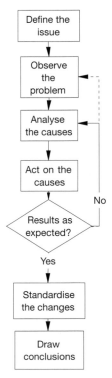

Input/Output flowcharts:

- Clearly identify inputs and outputs.
- Identify points for data collection; and show a focused view of process.

The inputs to the process are always shown on the left of the process step.

The outputs are shown on the right of the process step where they are produced.

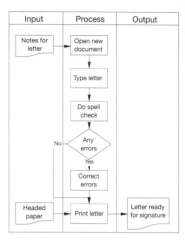

Integrated flowcharts combine the process and the organisational elements to give a clear picture of how they interact. An integrated flowchart:

- shows interaction of organisational elements;
- identifies customers/suppliers with the process;
- identifies points for data collection;
- provides clear overall view of the process.

Activity placed under a heading identifies responsibility for that action. If more than one organisational element is involved, the vertical line exiting the symbol indicates leadership responsibility.

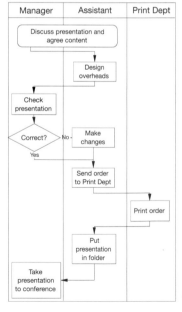

When an organisational element needs to be excluded from the activity a dotted line is used to show exclusion or non-responsibility.

Flowchart for producing an integrated flowchart

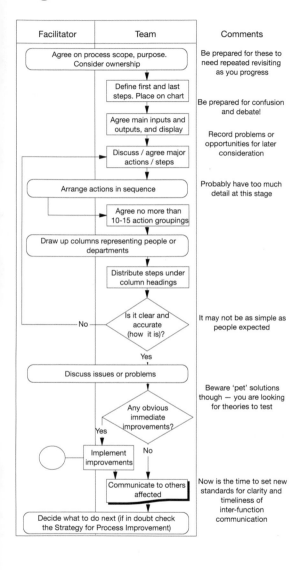

Facilitator	Team	Comments
Agree on process scope, purpose. Consider ownership		Be prepared for these to need repeated revisiting as you progress
	Define first and last steps. Place on chart	Be prepared for confusion and debate!
	Agree main inputs and outputs, and display	Record problems or opportunities for later consideration
	Discuss / agree major actions / steps	
Arrange actions in sequence		Probably have too much detail at this stage
	Agree no more than 10-15 action groupings	
Draw up columns representing people or departments		
	Distribute steps under column headings	
— No —	Is it clear and accurate (how it is)?	It may not be as simple as people expected
	Yes	
Discuss issues or problems		
	Any obvious immediate improvements?	Beware 'pet' solutions though — you are looking for theories to test
	Yes / No	
	Implement improvements	
	Communicate to others affected	Now is the time to set new standards for clarity and timeliness of inter-function communication
Decide what to do next (if in doubt check the Strategy for Process Improvement)		

Tips for facilitators

The following hints can help when facilitating a group which is drawing up a flowchart:

1. Keep exploring all inputs, outputs, customers and suppliers until you are satisfied you have everything. Only then prioritise for the level of detail to be included.
2. A comment column ensures that concerns and explanations are not lost.
3. The same person/department may be both a customer and supplier at different stages of the process. For instance, commercial customers both receive goods and supply money and information.
4. Don't put all the detail in. Use shadowed boxes to allow you to represent the process at the highest level appropriate to the team. Create flowcharts for sub-processes if useful. Only use a decision box if it is necessary to show such detail at that particular level of flowchart.
5. Keep your eye on the purpose of the process — that which is done for the real customer. All other outputs should be questioned for relevance and value.
6. Consider what data you could collect to show how well the process is running. The representation of delay steps indicates data collection opportunities.
7. Ensure everyone affected is present or has been consulted.
8. Be aware of different perspectives on the process, and record them – there may be no facts.
9. Start by flowcharting things as they actually are. Changes should follow understanding and be customer oriented.
10. Display draft flowcharts to enable others, who are affected but outside the active team, to contribute and become interested and involved.

Purpose of the process

Processes need to have explicit, shared purposes which are in harmony with the aim of the whole system. It may be useful to develop a shared vision for a process. The purpose:

- establishes why the process exists;
- should usually be evolved in conjunction with the customers of the process;
- must be clearly stated and understood by all who work in the process;
- remains constant even if the process is altered or improved.

The purpose needs to recognise interdependencies with neighbouring processes, so that improvements benefit the whole.

Process ownership

The process owner is ultimately accountable for overall process performance, co-ordination of all functions involved in the process, and ensuring it is capable of satisfying customers – meeting its purpose. Thus, process operators are able to work to the process in the confidence that the output will consistently be what is expected and needed.

The process owner has –

- ultimate accountability for the consistency of the output of the process;
- the authority to empower the people who work in the process to make changes to it;
- the responsibility for the entire process, for making improvements in that process, and for the repeatability of the results of the process.

A process owner must understand –

- what the process is supposed to do;
- how the process works;
- what the process is capable of producing.

This process knowledge will enable a process owner to –

- compare process performance against customer requirements (process capability);
- compare one process to others and assess priorities for improvement efforts.

A process owner sustains improvement efforts by –

- enabling learning by setting up, supporting, coaching, and encouraging team and individual efforts to improve;
- breaking down barriers to improvement;
- managing difficult boundaries, eg between departments.

The importance of the customer

The needs and wants of customers must be incorporated into the agreed process aim if the process is not to degenerate into unco-ordinated or competing parts. The customer should be recognised as a supplier of needs and wants and of information critical to the functioning of the process. If the customer is seen only as the recipient of whatever is produced, valuable time will be spent reacting to customer dissatisfaction.

Implications of an overall customer focus are:

- People in the process know their customers well.
- Customers contribute to process improvement efforts.
- Customer requirements are accurately expressed.
- Efforts are made to go beyond mere compliance with requirements to achieve delight.

Identifying and measuring customer requirements

It is imperative that organisations appreciate how their products and services look from their customers' point of view. This often requires a deliberate change in the words used to describe characteristics.

True quality characteristics are customer requirements stated in the customers' own words. They are valued product or service features such as safety, timeliness, and reliability. It is important that they are expressed in the customer's language – the voice of the customer. Often true quality characteristics cannot be measured directly.

Substitute quality characteristics are the measures a supplier uses to determine whether or not customer requirements are likely to be met – the voice of the process. Several substitute quality characteristics are often needed to check a single customer requirement. In this case it is important to understand the relationship between the true quality characteristic and the substitute quality characteristics. The matrix diagram (page 3-19) is a useful technique for this. See also Operational definitions (page 3-3 and following pages).

Suppliers

Concentration upon customer needs and wants should not obscure the key role of the supplier who is also part of the system. Constructive relations with suppliers enable understanding and reduction of the variation entering your processes at the same time as identification for cost reductions to benefit everyone.

Arrow diagram

The purpose of an arrow diagram is to establish a simple time sequenced action plan for completing a project or process. It provides a schedule for plans and a framework against which progress can be monitored. It has clear links with flowcharting of repeating processes and many of the questions and steps can be applied to flowcharts. Teams may want to assign one of their number to be competent in developing an arrow diagram with a software package. Starting with a simple method enables all to understand how times are calculated and progress monitored.

The arrow diagram helps to answer the following questions about an action plan or process.

1. Which steps can be eliminated from the plan (non-value added steps)?
2. Which steps should we work on to shorten completion time?
3. Which steps can be completed in parallel?

Developing an in-house training course

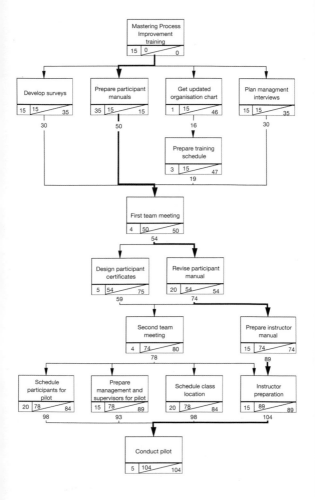

4. What is the expected project completion date?
5. What is the scheduled start and completion dates for each job?
6. Which jobs must be completed in the scheduled time so that the overall project will not be delayed?
7. Which jobs have flexible completion times?
8. How long can the completion of an activity be delayed without delaying the overall project?

Flowchart for an arrow diagram

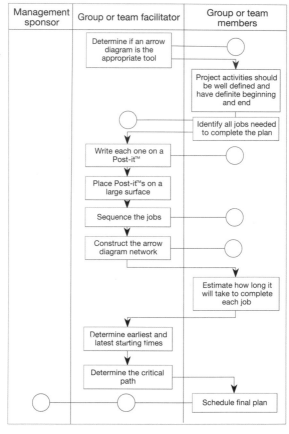

Management sponsor	Group or team facilitator	Group or team members

Process for producing an arrow diagram

1.   Generate a list of the tasks necessary to complete the plan.

2.   Write each task on a job card or Post-it™.

3.   Arrange the job cards in order.

     •   Ask 'Which tasks must be completed before we can do this one?' (sequential)

     •   Ask 'Which tasks can be completed while we do this one?' (parallel)

a.   It may be necessary to remove duplicate cards or add new ones as you discover gaps.

b.   When the cards are arranged, assign each task a letter and write it on the job card.

c.   In drawing the arrow diagram, you may use the cards themselves, or substitute nodes (circles) for cards and reference the tasks in a table.

d. Draw solid lines with arrows from each job card to the one immediately following it.

4. Estimate how long it will take to complete each job.

5. Record the estimated time to complete each task on the bottom of the job card.

6. Determine the earliest and latest start times for each activity.

    a. Beginning at the first activity, calculate the earliest time each task could be started (EST). Write that number on the job card. Continue to the last card.

    b. Beginning at the last activity, determine the latest time (LST) each task could be started and still finish the project on schedule. Write that number below the EST.

Any difference between the EST and LST of a task is the slack time for that task. Those tasks for which EST = LST form the critical path.

Determine the critical path by finding which path has the longest completion time from start to end. This tells you how long it will take you to complete the project.

7. Schedule dates for final plan and put the dates on the arrow diagram.

Tips for facilitators

1. Don't make it more complex than it needs to be. For example, minor activities that are unlikely to affect the schedule may not need to be listed.

2. Like a flowchart, some of the larger, more complex activities that appear as a single activity may need to be broken down and expanded with their own arrow diagram or flowchart.

3. Don't be optimistic with completion times. Three scenarios may be calculated: optimistic, most likely, and worst case completion times.

4. Once the ESTs and LSTs have been calculated, put in actual start dates or times.

5. Don't allow the complexity built into most PERT/CPM computer programs to bog you down. Keep it simple.

6. A Gantt chart can be used to show time relationships of these tasks; however, it masks any sequential dependencies.

7. A copy may be taken of the form without the EST/LST times, to be used to update the project as it progresses

Contingency analysis

Processes and projects sometimes go wrong! Small decisions can have large consequences, often distant in both time and space. Process flowcharts or project plans should be examined for possible problems in a systematic manner. A process decision programme chart (PDPC) analysis develops contingency plans for either –

1. preventing or dealing with potential problems before they arise; or
2. recovering quickly from problems that do arise.

It is similar to failure modes and effects analysis (FMEA) and fault tree analysis (FTA). Some organisations find that a simple fishbone diagram, turned to face the left, can be useful and they refer to it as a solution effect diagram.

The cloud graphics are used partly to denote the rather indefinite nature of the issues, and also serve to distinguish a PDPC from a systematic diagram used in analysing actions (page 3-15).

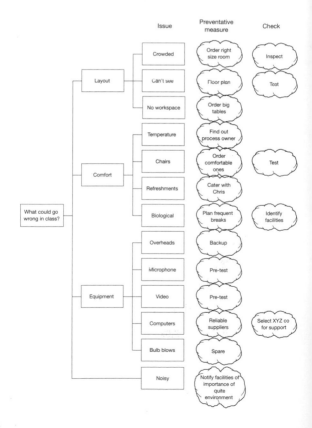

How to construct a PDPC

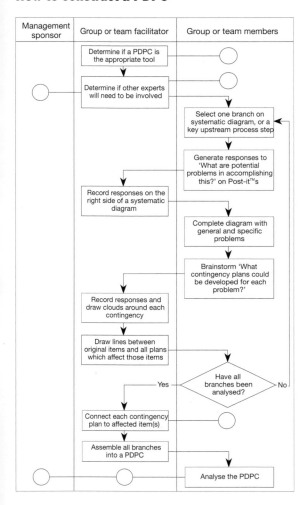

Process

1. When starting from a systematic diagram select one of the leftmost branches. Brainstorm a list of potential problems that could arise while accomplishing this objective. Each major branch could generate its own systematic diagram.

2. Record the problems to the right of the brainstorm question. Cluster them as with the systematic diagram.

3. When you have broken down the general problems to specific root causes, brainstorm contingency plans for each of them. Record the contingency plans opposite the appropriate spot on the PDPC. (Enclose them in small clouds.)

4. Continue as above until all branches of the systematic diagram (or steps in the process flowchart) have been analysed. You may choose to anticipate further problems by deciding what to do if your preventative measures do not succeed and mitigating action is called for.

5. Connect each contingency plan to the items which will be affected by the plan.

6. If all the contingency plans cannot be carried out, prioritise them. Consider the following:
   - Probability of occurrence
   - Severity (or consequences)
   - Resources needed to carry out the plan

7. Alternative approaches may be considered when discussing a PDPC:
   - 1: Preventative design
   - 2: Damage limitation

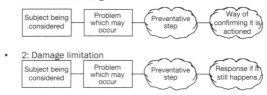

Tips for facilitators

1. Use the same approach as with the systematic diagram to divide the main concerns into categories of potential problems. However, a team may be comfortable with a cause and effect diagram format.

2. Work on only one issue at a time or the discussion will lose focus.

3. If only a subset of the potential problems can be dealt with, use probability and severity of occurrence, and resources required to prioritise them. (The risk from a potential problem may be calculated by risk = [probability of occurrence] x [severity if it occurs].)

4. Process or subject matter experts should be brought in to help brainstorm potential problems or to develop countermeasures.

5. As an aid to brainstorming potential problems, use a high level flowchart or arrow diagram and ask 'What could go wrong or hinder the team in this step?'

6. A PDPC often generates an explosion of ideas which can be overwhelming. The level of effort spent on a PDPC depends on the importance of the project and the likelihood of setbacks.

7. Ensure contingency plans are reasonable to implement.

8. Share results with sponsors of the team and/or customers.

Developing a SIPOC

The SIPOC diagram will help provide an overall summary of the process under study. This high-level view contains –

- a linear flowchart of the process;
- customers and their requirements;
- suppliers and inputs;
- measures both (leading – Process, and lagging – Results);
- present performance of the portions of the process; and
- initial theories (unsubstantiated) on the sources of variation and how this impacts the business.

The SIPOC can be very useful for the team in providing –

- an intial view of the process and its performance in the generation of their contract; and
- a single page summary of their view of the process and its status for communication and reviews.

It does not replace the need for a full linear and integrated flow chart as defined in Process Definition, but has its place as a very effective communications tool.

SIPOC Diagram

Key Business Process: Pizza Ordering and Delivery Process

Created by: The PP Project Team

Suppliers	Inputs	Process	Outputs	Customers
Dough-R-us Clients Market Presto pizza	Dough Telephone order Ingredients kitchen	**Name:** Order and deliver a pizza **Purpose:** to deliver a pizza to a customer **Owner:** Luigi Tartufi	Pizza Bill Empty cartons Dirty baking trays	Delivery driver The end customer Kitchen staff

Key Business Process: Pizza Ordering and Delivery Process

								Results Measures
								On time delivery from phone order to receipt of pizza
Process Steps	Take telephone order	Take order to chef	Make pizza	Cook pizza	Hand to delivery guy	Drive to customer	Present pizza and bill	**Customer Needs**
								Total time delivery within 30 minutes
Process Measures	Number of rings before answering	Time taken to give to chef	Time to make a pizza	Time to cook a pizza	Number of pizzas given to delivery guy	Time taken to drive to customer	Time waiting for customer to open door	Hot pizza Not over cooked not undercooked Right toppings Friendly delivery driver with enough cash
Present Data	none	none	none	none	none	none	92 late deliveries this month	
Goal Performance	Within 3 rings	none	none	<12 minutes	none	20 minutes	Total time <30 minutes	**Results Concerns**
								Late delivery means half the money back
Sources of Variation or Waste	Busy in restaurant, not enough staff	Busy chef	Backlog in preparation	Oven temperature	Availability of a driver	Availability of a driver Traffic jams, ease of directions	Customer waiting to open door	**Date:**
Impact on	Time delay,	Time delay	Under/over	Late delivery,	Going over 30		**Version:**

Construction of a SIPOC

- Identify the process under investigation.
- Define the purpose of the process.
  - Why does this process exist?
- Record the Process Owner (if known).
  - Who has accountability for the whole process?
- Clarify the boundaries of the process (start and stop steps)
  - Where does the process start and finish?
- List key outputs and customers.
  - What product/service does the process provide?
  - Who are the users of the output of the process
- List key inputs and suppliers.
  - What information/material is used in the process?
  - Who supplies the information/material used in the process?
- Define the major process steps and their order (see Linear Flowcharts section of Process Definition for more details).
  - What happens to the inputs at each step?
- Define Lagging (Results) and Leading (Process) measures.
  - What measures indicate that the customer's needs have been met?
  - What measures in the process indicate that the final results measures will be acceptable?
- Identify present performance of process and needed performance.
  - How is the process performing today?
  - Where should the performance be to meet fully the customer's needs?
  - What is the present process DPMO and process sigma?
- Define initial thoughts on the cause for the inadequate performance and how they impact the process.
  - What theories exist about the causes of poor performance?
  - How does this variation impact the performace of the operation?
  - How does this performace impact the business financially?
  - How does this performance impact the time to produce the product of provide the service?

Having the whole team working together at this very early stage to complete the SIPOC will provide them with a common view of the process and the problem, and will mean that they are more likely to move forward together.

On Target with Minimum Variation

Variation may be introduced by many factors: materials, people, environment, equipment, and the methods used in the work – the process itself. Once introduced into the system, variation interacts and multiplies, affecting everything downstream. The process manager seeks first to understand how the work is done – the processes and the system, and then how variation affects these processes, the organisation and its customers. This section describes some tools which provide systematic ways of collecting and interpreting data to facilitate learning and appropriate action. The aim is to get processes 'On Target with Minimum Variation'.

The tools should be used in the context of the PDSA (Plan – Do – Study – Act) cycle. (See page 3-2.)

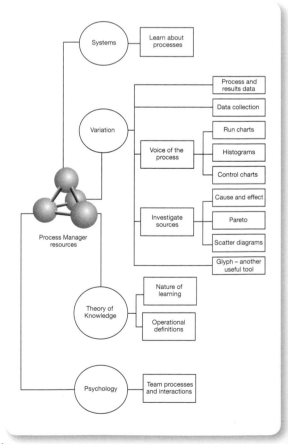

Collecting data

Data collection should be planned after some study of the process and its customers and suppliers. Operational definitions provide guidance on what will be appropriate. (page 3-3)

Purpose

Data provide a means to form or test theories about a process. Collection involves combining sampling techniques with a data collection sheet to ensure that the data obtained are appropriate to the subject. Useful data may be collected both from processes being run experimentally and those in routine operation.

Hints on collecting data

Flowcharting often exposes opportunities for collecting data which would be useful in monitoring and improvement–process data. There are also requirements for reporting to management or customers—results data. In either case the data must be as accurate as possible, and bear these rules in mind:

* Collect data just in time — not just in case!
* Let the theory indicate what data to collect; don't let the data dictate the theory to be tested.
* For data to provide useful information about an operation, they need to be taken at that operation, not remotely.
* Focus on the data to reduce finger-pointing.
* Choose methods and forms that will minimise bias.

A moderate amount of carefully collected data used immediately is worth more than lots of thoughtless data that are never used!

Bias in data collection

Bias is a distortion in a measurement or response. It can stem from the sampling technique, data collection sheet, interviewer or observer, the measurement process or environmental conditions. Be aware of potential biases and plan to remove them or, if they can't be eliminated, acknowledge them.

Types of data

Qualitative data are non-numerical data or information, whilst quantitative data are numerical and can be of two types:

* Attributes data: counts about the presence or absence of some feature or condition
* Variables data: measurements of some characteristic

Variables data provide more detail and produce better analysis than attributes data and should be gathered whenever possible.

Measures for monitoring the process

R-Criteria and P-Criteria: an important distinction

'True' quality characteristics are those that relate to the customer's requirements (page 1-10).

Substitute quality characteristics (see Operational definitions page 3-3) provide critical customer-driven measures to monitor process performance. These measures are typically results-oriented (R-Criteria) and help quantify the history and current state of the process. However, upstream measures give more insight into what is causing the process to vary and are referred to as P-Criteria.

R-Criteria, tied to end results or outcomes of the process, have the following characteristics:

* overall process performance measures;
* useful to prioritise areas for improvement and monitor process improvement efforts;
* enable a shared understanding of the present state;
* indirect measures of customer requirements;
* fairly easy to identify;
* reporting them may not lead to improvement.

P-Criteria measure factors found in the process and have the following characteristics:

* tied to the process, correlated with the output;
* indicate elements of the process, which if done consistently and successfully will ensure the right results;
* may be difficult to identify at the beginning;
* finding them may not yield immediate results;
* focus on the long term;
* indicate where action to improve needs to be taken;
* manageable by people in the process.

Discussing P-Criteria helps a transformation from judging and justifying historic performances of people, and excuses for shortfalls, to analysing process behaviours for future improvement.

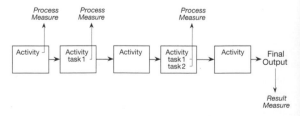

Sampling

- Sampling provides data to serve as a basis for action, either on a process or on the output produced by the process.
- Sampling is less expensive and time consuming than measuring all items.
- Careful sampling will usually provide sufficient information.
- Sampling is essential when measurement requires the destruction of the product.

When taking samples be aware of the sampling method and how representative of the process being studied the sample is likely to be.

General rules for data collection

1. Clearly define the purpose for collecting data.
   - Determine the purpose first, for that has a major influence on what is collected.
   - Determine what you will do with data after you have collected it as this should control how it is done.

2. Use a data collection sheet, making sure it is clear and easy to fill out.

3. PDSA the data collection method on a small scale in order to:
   - ensure you are getting what you expect.
   - confirm the usefulness of the form.

4. Document the methods comprehensively so that others can repeat them.

5. Follow a set procedure in data collection, giving specific instructions for collection.

6. Collect all applicable data the first time, so you don't have to repeat the process.

7. Be prepared for displayed data to influence that which is being recorded!

Questions to ask before sampling

Why – collect data?

What   – actions will be taken as a result?
         – characteristics will be studied?
         – type of data will be gathered?
         – will be the effect of collecting the data?

Data collection sheets

Data collection sheets should be well documented and designed to be easy to complete and analyse.

The print size needs to be readable and the instructions must be easy to understand. Both the tally or recording area and documentation spaces should be large enough for everything
to fit inside.

Basic parts of a data collection sheet/form.

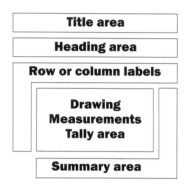

There are three main types of data collection sheets:

- A drawing can be used to show the location of errors or nonconformaties that are found on a sample of items.
  A drawing can be very useful when recording attribute data.
- A sheet for listing the data measurements (variables) as they are received.
- A sheet which allows attributes data to be tallied into identified groupings.

Checklist for the team to agree and communicate:

Who?   – Who will take observations?
            – Who is the customer of these data?
            – Who will analyse the data?
            – Who will communicate what to whom?

When?   – How frequently will samples be collected?

Where?   – Where in the process will observations be taken?

How?   – What measurement methods will be used?
            – How will the data be analysed?

Listening to the voice of the process

The simple quality tools enable us to listen to the voice of the process. The only way the process 'speaks' is through the data collected. When using the tools, anticipate the questions a visitor would ask about axes, definitions, scales, which way is 'good', and so on. The less time spent on discussion of what is being shown, the quicker you can get to what is to be done to improve.

Run charts
Purpose
As a process improvement tool, run charts allow for the observation of a process characteristic while preserving the time order of the data.

Run chart

Run charts show changes in a process over time by giving an indication of:

- the centre and spread of the process;
- recurring cycles, trends, or shifts;
- the effects of changes over time.

Run charts can be used for variables and attributes data.

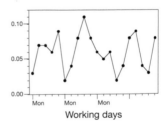

Proportion of Invoices with at least one error

Run chart construction
The following are key steps for constructing a run chart.

1. Draw horizontal and vertical axes.
2. Label the horizontal axis 'time'.
3. Label the vertical axis with the characteristic being measured.
4. Label tick marks to identify the respective units of measurement.
5. Ideally, you should enter the data on the chart as soon as they are collected.
6. Connect the points.

Run charts may not be reliable indicators of process stability — for that one needs control charts. (See page 2-13 and following pages.)

Shape, centre, and spread

Statistical concepts related to shape, centre, and spread help
individuals learn about processes, how to diagnose problems with
processes, and understand process stability.

Histograms

Histograms can be used to describe a data set with
respect to shape, centre, and spread. Histograms
alone cannot indicate whether the process that
generates the data is stable, for there is no time
element.

Histograms:

* Illustrate shape, centre, and spread of a stable process.
* Show what a stable process is capable of producing.
* Help identify sorting, rework, or multiple sources of variation in a
  process.

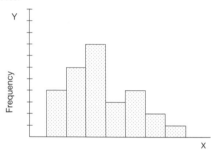

Histogram construction

Step 1:   Determine the approximate number of classes

Classes are categories defined by lower and upper boundaries; they
are used to group observations.

The desired number of classes is variable and depends primarily on
the quantity of data. It is probably better to have too many
than too few.

Use the following table as a guide for determining the number of
classes.

No. of data points	No. of classes
0-32	5
33-64	6
65-128	7
129-256	8

eep in mind that when the original data are grouped into classes,
he information is lost.

Step 2:   Establish class width and boundaries

Class width

All classes should be the same size or width. The formula to calculate class width is as follows:

$$\text{Class Width} = \frac{\text{the largest observation} - \text{the smallest observation}}{\text{the approximate number of classes}}$$

Class boundaries

When establishing class boundaries, keep the following guidelines in mind.

- Choose class boundaries which are easy to use.
- Begin by specifying the lower boundary of the class containing the smallest values.
- Successively add the class width to get the other class boundaries.
- Be unambiguous about boundaries to avoid possible class overlap.

Step 3:   Tally the observations

1. Establish column headings for tally and frequency.
2. In the tally column, record each observation with a tally on the row of the appropriate class.
3. In the frequency column, record the number of tallies for each class and then total them.

Step 4:   Plot the histogram

1. On the horizontal axis (x), mark the class boundaries or, if the scale does not begin at zero, indicate that with a break in the horizontal axis.
2. Scale the vertical axis (y) to show frequencies so as to accommodate the highest frequency. The vertical scale must begin at zero.
3. Using the scale on the vertical axis (y) plot vertical bars above each class corresponding to the frequency of occurrence.

Shape

Having an understanding of the shape of the data produced by the process helps in the development of theories to explain what is happening, diagnosing problems, and identifying sources of variation.

Centre

Measures of centre may be used to partially characterise a data set by a single number. They provide the options for the centre line on a control chart.

Definition of mean

The mean, $\bar{X}$, represents the balance point of a data set – the sample mean.

Calculating the mean

Let $x_1, x_2, x_3, \ldots\ldots x_n$ represent the sample values where n is the number of values in the sample. The mean is calculated by adding up all the values and dividing the total by n.

Definition of median

The median is the middle number of a set of data: half of the numbers are larger than the median, and half are smaller.

The median is less sensitive to extreme values than the mean.

Calculating the sample median

To calculate the sample median:

1. Arrange the data values in ascending or descending order.
2. For n observations do the following:
   - if n is odd, the median is the middle number; and
   - if n is even, the median is the average of the two middle numbers.

Spread

Measures of spread provide an indication of the magnitude of variability in a data set. They are used, along with a measure of centre, to construct control limits.

Just as the mean and median measure centre differently, the range and standard deviation measure spread differently.

Definition of range

The range (R) is the difference between the largest and smallest values in the data set.

Calculating the range

$R = X_{max} - X_{min}$

- The range is zero when there is no variability in a set of data.
- The range is based on extreme values.

Definition of standard deviation

The standard deviation, s, can be thought of as an average deviation of individual data values from the mean.

- The standard deviation takes into account the value of individual observations in the sample as opposed to the range which uses the two extreme data points, ie, the maximum and minimum values.
- Standard deviations can be compared even when calculated from different sample sizes.
- There are various methods for estimating the standard deviation of a process depending on whether you are interested in only common cause variation or total variation.

Total variation

When calculating the total variation in a process, use the Root Mean Squared (RMS) method to calculate standard deviation.

Calculating total variation using RMS method

- Calculate the mean, $\bar{X}$, of the n observations.
- Subtract the sample mean, $\bar{X}$, from each of the n individual observations to create n deviations.
- Square each of the n deviations to create n squared-deviations.
- Sum the n squared-deviations to get the sum-of-squares.
- Divide the sum-of-squares by $n-1$ to get the variance.
- Get the standard deviation by taking the square root of the variance.

Control charts have upper and lower control limits to identify the extremes of typical common cause variation in the process.
By using the range of anticipated common cause variation, the chart is sensitive to assignable causes.

The RMS method of calculating standard deviation includes the variation arising from both common and assignable causes.
A method to separate out the common cause variation is needed.

This is done by:

- Splitting the data into short subgroups
- Calculating the range of each subgroup
- Calculating the average range over all the subgroups ($\bar{R}$, pronounced R-bar)
- Making an adjustment to correct the range for sample size (d_2)
- Basing the estimate of standard deviation on this 'corrected' $\bar{R}$

Splitting the data into subgroups reduces the sensitivity of the estimated standard deviation to assignable cause variation.

The empirical rule

The empirical rule describes what percentage of data values fall within one, two, and three standard deviations of the mean (average). It applies for almost any set of data.

Part 1:   Roughly 60 to 75 per cent of the data will be located within the distance of one standard deviation on either side of the mean.

Part 2:   Usually 90 to 98 per cent of the data will be located within the distance of two standard deviations on either side of the mean.

Part 3:   Approximately 99 to 100 per cent of the data will be located within a distance of three standard deviations on either side of the mean.

Loss functions

The traditional view of quality, conformance to specification, can lead to the belief that any product falling between the upper and lower specification limits is 'good' and any falling outside these limits is 'no-good'. The loss is assumed to be zero as long as the product falls within the specification limits.

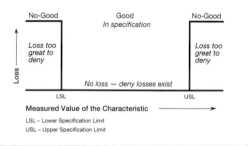

Taguchi used a more realistic diagram to represent the loss function. The loss is at its lowest, but not necessarily zero, when the quality characteristic is on target. Loss gradually increases as the distance from the target increases.

This type of double-sided loss function does not apply in all circumstances:

* A service/delivery required as soon as possible.
* A level of a chemical specified as 'less than 100ppm' – then smaller is better.

Taguchi Loss Function

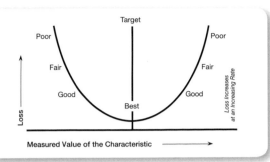

Process stability

All process and results data exhibit variation. Reducing this variation is a key improvement target. The sources of the variation in the data can be usefully categorised into two types:

Common causes – faults of the system, due to random variation inherent in the design of the process and its operation. Management has the prime responsibility to discover and eliminate these causes with the help of those working in the process.

Assignable causes – created by changes that have occurred in the inputs or operation of the process that are not common. Identification and removal of these causes is best done by those closest to the process. Management may need to provide support.

A process is said to be stable when only common cause variation is present. It is important to remember this because:

- An unstable process is unpredictable.
- Removing sources of instability is the first step to improving an unstable process.
- The presence of assignable causes makes identification and reduction of common causes more difficult.

Processes operating with occurrences of assignable causes are said to be out of control or unstable. Such processes cannot be predicted reliably either in terms of mean or spread.

None of these terms in any way relates to customer requirements. Unstable processes, however good in recent history, are risky processes to operate in terms of confidence in meeting customer requirements. Stable processes are therefore favoured but to be valuable they must also be operating close to the target with appropriately low common cause variation.

Failure to recognise the significance of the two different types of variation can lead to decisions which result in over-adjustment or over-reaction, known as tampering. If the process is stable the effect of such action is to increase variation. Making matters worse by tampering is a common mistake and a major source of waste and increased cost.

Control charts provide an operational definition (see page 3-3) of which type of process is operating.

Control charts

Control charts were invented in the 1920s by Walter Shewhart. They are used to detect opportunities to learn, in other words when assignable causes are affecting the process. Consistently learning from and then removing assignable causes leads to continual improvement.

Control chart

The process is monitored through time and the points are plotted on the chart.

- Control charts help identify when a process is stable and thus operating under common causes of variation – a consistent, or predictable process.
- Control limits indicate the expected variation in the value monitored.
- The control chart enables people in processes to identify, and then eliminate, assignable causes of variation.
- The attainment of process stability is an achievement. It does not just happen. The job then becomes one of forever reducing the effects of the common causes of variation.
- A stable process may not produce output that is acceptable – but reacting to individual points will probably make it worse (tampering, see above).
- A process must be stable before the concept of standard deviation of the process data is meaningful.
- The empirical rule (see page 2-11) applies to all distributions regardless of their shape.

Selecting an appropriate chart

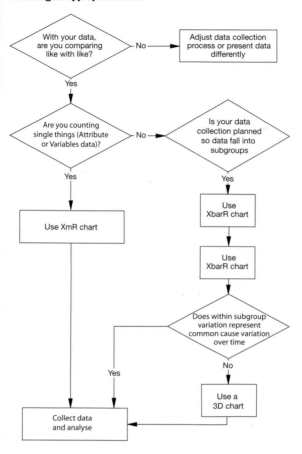

Walter Shewhart developed a set of theories for defining process stability. They are based on empirical — practical — tests, and calculated using the three standard deviations for common causes of variation. This is simple, and gives a very low chance of a false indication. Applying more detailed statistical rules complicates matters and does not usually help the operator or manager come to better decisions overall.

There are many types of control charts, but they all have the same basic parts, appearance, and decision rules:

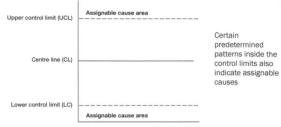

You should ideally, collect 20-25 data points before calculating a control chart.

Individuals charts (XmR or ImR)

Use individuals charts if the following conditions apply:

1. Data are variables.
2. Data occur singly (eg, daily yields, monthly sales, periodic comparison between forecast and actual figures), or do not fall naturally into subgroups.

In practice, you will find that individuals charts will often be useful even if you are not exactly sure of the nature of the data. They are particularly useful for many types of management and service data, especially in comparing the difference between a forecast figure and the actual result.

Individuals data are used to construct the individuals and moving range (XmR) chart. The estimate of variation is obtained by comparing adjacent values. The difference between all pairs of adjacent values is calculated. These differences are called the 'moving ranges' and are always taken as positive.

Individuals moving range formulae

Individuals chart
Centre line: $\overline{X}$ = mean of individual values
Upper control limit: $UCL_x = \overline{X} + 2.66\overline{R}$
Lower control limit: $LCL_x = \overline{X} - 2.66\overline{R}$

Moving range chart
Centre line: $\overline{R}$ = mean of the moving range values
Upper control limit: $UCL_R = 3.27\overline{R}$
Lower control limit: $LCL_R = 0.0\overline{R} = 0$

The lower control limit is, therefore, not useful for signalling assignable causes and need not be displayed.

Interpretation of individuals and moving range charts

- The two charts are highly interdependent and the same signal often shows in both.
- A change in location of the mean is easiest seen in the individuals chart. However, a change in location will usually cause at least one relatively large R value.
- A change in variation is best seen in the R chart. However:
  - increased variation increases the chance of low and high values in the individuals chart.
  - reduced variation should be associated with X values grouped closer to the centre line.

  For these reasons, we recommend that you plot both charts and interpret them together. Use two rules A+B suggested on page 2-20.

General points to consider in using individuals/moving range charts:

- Charts for moving ranges can sometimes be difficult to interpret because consecutive ranges are always dependent and this dependency must be taken into account.
- Charts for individuals are not very sensitive to small shifts or gradual trends in the process average. It may take a while for a chart to pick up a trend or a shift, and you will need to look for a possible cause back at the start of the run of eight points. Go back as far as the last time it crossed the centre line.
- When assignable causes are indicated, they should always be investigated.
- Although individuals charts are suggested for variables data, they will often be the best choice also for attributes data.
- As is the case with all control charts, an individuals chart indicating that the process is stable does not necessarily mean that the output is acceptable or the process capable.

Relationship between control limits and the histogram

For individuals data, if the histogram of the plotted points were tipped on its side it would fall between the control limits on the control chart. It is useful to get into the habit of imagining this histogram when trying to understand the behaviour of a process.

$\overline{X}$ and R charts ($\overline{X}$/R)

$\overline{X}$ and R charts are used to monitor and control the variability of a quality characteristic that is monitored using variables data that falls naturally into subgroups.

Notation

n: Number of measurements in each subgroup.

$\overline{R}$:   Average of the ranges.

$\overline{\overline{X}}$:   Average of the subgroup averages.

D_4:   Tabular constant used for R chart UCL. (See below.)

D_3:   Tabular constant used for R chart LCL.

A_2:   Tabular constant used for $\overline{X}$ chart LCL and UCL.

Factors for variables control charts

Tabled values used depend on the value of n, the subgroup size.

n	A_2	D_3	D_4	d_2
2	1.88	0	3.27	1.128
3	1.02	0	2.57	1.693
4	0.73	0	2.28	2.059
5	0.58	0	2.11	2.326
6	0.48	0	2.00	2.534
7	0.42	0.08	1.92	2.704

When to use $\overline{X}$ and R charts

1. Data are variables.
2. Each measurement is independent of the other measurements (ie, the result of one observation doesn't influence the result of another).
3. The output of the process naturally falls into subgroups (ie, one can take a small sample over a small interval of time).

Formulae

The following formulae are used to calculate the limits and centre line for R charts and $\overline{X}$ charts.

$\overline{X}$ Chart

Centre line: $\overline{\overline{X}}$ = mean of the subgroup means
Upper control limit: $UCL_{\overline{x}} = \overline{\overline{X}} + A_2\overline{R}$
Lower control limit: $LCL_{\overline{x}} = \overline{\overline{X}} - A_2\overline{R}$
Note: $UCL_{\overline{x}}$ and $LCL_{\overline{x}}$ are sometimes expressed as: $\overline{\overline{X}} \pm A_2\overline{R}$

R Chart

Centre line: $\overline{R}$ = mean of the subgroup ranges
Upper control limit: $UCL_R = D_4\overline{R}$
Lower control limit: $LCL_R = D_3\overline{R}$

Interpretation of $\overline{X}$ and R charts

The $\overline{X}$ and R charts should be interpreted together. When a chart is based on a learning set the implications of the interpretation will be slightly different to when charts are operating live.

Changes in process centre will primarily be indicated by a signal in the $\overline{X}$ chart. Such changes will only affect the R values if the change occurred within a subgroup.

Changes in variation will be indicated by signals in the R chart. However, increased variation will lead to an increased chance of extreme $\overline{X}$ values. Occasionally therefore, increased variation can be signalled first in the $\overline{X}$ chart or simultaneously in both charts.

Usually reduced variation will be signalled by a run of low R values. However, this should normally be accompanied by the $\overline{X}$ values keeping more closely to their centre line. A stable $\overline{X}$ chart does not necessarily mean that the output is acceptable.

It is important to note that control limits for $\overline{X}$ are not the same as the natural limits for individual outcomes from the process.

Note: Signals on charts indicate that there may be assignable causes of variation. Seek to understand the source of these assignable causes and learn from them. Where such causes can be confirmed in data collected during the learning phase, it will probably be worth recalculating the control limits and then re-evaluating the charts.

3D Charts

3D charts should be used if your process knowledge (perhaps gained through trying to use an $\overline{X}/R$ chart) indicates that the within subgroup variation is not a useful estimate of common cause variation for between subgroup means. Use the following process for their calculation.

1. Decide that this is the appropriate chart.
2. Calculate subgroup means and ranges as for an $\overline{X}/R$ chart.
3. Calculate $\overline{\overline{X}}$ and $\overline{R}$ from the subgroup values.
4. Calculate the moving ranges for the subgroup means.
5. Calculate the mean of the moving ranges.
6. Create an individuals chart using the subgroup means and the mean moving range of the subgroup means.
7. Create a moving range chart linked to the individuals chart.
8. Create a range chart in the same way as for the $\overline{X}/R$ chart.
9. Interpret the results.
10. Use 'Live'.

Control chart decision rules

Use the following guidelines to detect assignable causes of variation.
We recommend that you do not add significantly to
these rules.

Rule A: One point above the UCL or below the LCL

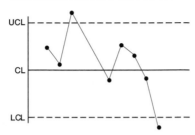

Rule B: Eight points, or more, in a row above or below the
centre line

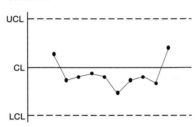

- 16 consecutive points are alternating up and down.
- Other consistent patterns should also trigger interest. A pattern
  repeating 8 times is a useful rule of thumb.

Beware! It is all too easy to over interpret data and to frame
happenstance variation as a repeating pattern. If you believe you have
detected a repeating pattern write down an operational definition
of the pattern and only interpret subsequent sequences as signals
of possible assignable causes. Do not use the same data to build a
theory and to test it.

Summary

Consider the following in clarifying the relationship between process stability, prediction, and planning.

- Planning requires prediction.
- When a process is stable there is a rational basis for predicting future output.
- Results which are inconsistent with the prediction indicate a learning opportunity.
- Being stable does not mean that all output is acceptable. Control limits are **not** specification limits!

Control charts are created from a learning set of data (approx. 24 data points) and then used to monitor new data set. The actual use of the charts is on new data as they are plotted — new control limits are best recalculated only when there is evidence of an assignable cause, the change is sustained, the change is an improvement, and you know what caused the change.

Process Capability

Process capability is a method of assessing the level of confidence in the ability of the process to meet customer requirements as expressed by specifications. The value is also useful as a means of summarising the status of different processes, in order to prioritise improvement efforts. It requires –

- meaningful customer requirements – 'voice of the customer'; (see page 2-3)
- knowledge of the process performance – 'voice of the process'; (see page 2-6)
- a suitable and stable measurement process; and
- careful interpretation.

It helps in addressing the question, 'Will the output from the process stay within the specification limits?', to consider three separate questions:

1. Is the output predictable (stable)? (See page 2-12)
2. Is the expected variation in output less than that allowed by the specification?
3. Where is the process centred?

The following are definitions relevant to process capability calculations.

The **process centre** is the centre line of the current control chart:

$\overline{X}$ for an individuals chart, or $\overline{\overline{X}}$ for an $\overline{X}/R$ chart.

Natural tolerance (NT): The natural tolerance of a process is taken to be $6s_x$ where s_x is an estimate of the common cause, standard deviation of the individuals in a stable process.

To calculate the natural tolerance use:

$$6\frac{\overline{R}}{d_2} \qquad \text{see page 2-17 for table of } d_2 \text{ values.}$$

This can also be directly calculated from the control limits.

For an individuals chart, NT is equal to $(UCL_x - LCL_x)$

For an $\overline{X}$ chart, NT is equal to $\sqrt{n}\,(UCL_{\overline{x}} - LCL_{\overline{x}})$

Note: This is wider than the control limits for $\overline{X}/R$ charts.

Engineering tolerance (ET): The engineering tolerance is the amount of variation allowed by the specifications, where USL is the upper, and LSL is the lower, specification limit. Whilst this is the term conventionally used, a specification can be agreed with a customer of any product or service. In this case, simply use the width of the agreed specification.

Process capability indices –

- can only be as good as the engineering tolerance (specifications);
- should be supported by control charts showing that the process is stable;
- are only an estimate and therefore should be interpreted conservatively; and
- cannot guarantee that all output will be acceptable at the point of use (as many other factors can intervene).

Formulae

C_p — an index of the capability of the natural tolerance of the process in relation to the engineering tolerance.

$$C_p = \frac{(USL - LSL)}{6s_x} \quad \text{or} \quad \frac{ET}{NT}$$

C_p ignores where the process is centred so we need an index which allows for centring.

C_{pk} — an index of the capability of half the NT in relation to the relevant specification limit.

$$C_{pk} \text{ upper} = \frac{(USL - \overline{\overline{X}})}{3s_x} \qquad C_{pk} \text{ lower} = \frac{(\overline{\overline{X}} - LSL)}{3s_x}$$

The lower of the two values is the quoted capability index.

A capable process will be stable and has a C_{pk} which is greater than or equal to one.

Capability recalculation is only justified when control limit recalculation is justified, that is when common cause variation is shown to have changed. Control charts monitor the process and provide signals for learning how to reduce variation. Do not use process capability as a substitute or an addition.

How to use capability indices

The main use of capability indices is in prioritising improvement efforts between different processes or customer defined characteristics; however, the values do provide some insight.

- Large is good, small is bad.
- A value of 1.0 is a crude threshold.
- Below 1.0, expect to deliver unsatisfactory product or service. The level of dissatisfaction grows quickly as the index reduces from 1.0.
- Close to 1.0 there is no scope for even minor drift in the process centre before dissatisfaction will rise.
- Values of 2.0 and above are comforting, but do not become complacent; maintenance of stability and capability requires relentless attention and appropriate interpretation of control charts.

Investigating sources of variation

Cause and effect diagrams

Cause and effect diagrams (*Ishikawa* or fishbone diagrams) can be used to generate and sort several potential causes of variation within a process. They are less useful for analysing large scale, systems level problems, when some of the *Seven Management and Planning Tools* should be used (Section 3).

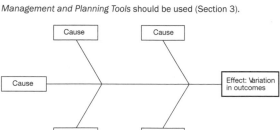

Cause and Effect

Benefits of cause and effect diagrams

*   Simple to use.
*   Help form theories.
*   Help sort out possible sources of variation or causes of problems.
*   Provide systematic approach to problem-solving.
*   Help document ideas and theories.
*   Get everyone involved in a team effort.

Almost everyone has been involved in brainstorming sessions where ideas are generated but little action is taken. Cause and effect diagrams get everyone involved and working as a team, help guide discussions, and keep participants focused on the issue at hand.

When using cause and effect diagrams, a team is able to –

*   reveal complex sets of elements that might be possible causes of a problem;
*   identify areas for further data collection to improve a process;
*   generate possible solutions; and
*   document theories or ideas.

Cause and effect diagram construction

Five major cause categories are typically labelled as follows:

*   Materials
*   Methods
*   Equipment
*   Environment
*   People

Note: Other headings may also be used.

Each of these major cause categories is broken down into as many categories or sub-categories as needed. These will appear as twigs or branches of the fishbone.

To construct a cause and effect diagram, follow the rules for idea generation and the steps for constructing and acting upon a cause and effect diagram provided below.

1. Define the problem clearly. It is often useful to express it in terms of 'What sources of variation affect....?'.
2. Decide on the main cause categories.
3. Idea generation for each cause category.
4. Record ideas on a cause and effect diagram.
5. Clarify the meaning of each idea; distil the list.
6. Rank the ideas for the most likely cause.
7. Develop action items to check the most likely causes by study and data collection.
8. Display the diagram and encourage contribution from others involved but not in the team.

Idea generation rules
1. Encourage spontaneous, freewheeling responses.
2. Do not discuss each other's ideas.
3. Cultivate a supportive atmosphere.
4. Emphasise quantity, not quality.
5. Build on the ideas of others.
6. Write everything down.
7. Seek total participation from the group.
8. Discourage non-verbal responses to ideas.

Pareto diagrams

Pareto diagrams indicate priorities for problem investigation or the main sources of variation. The basis for prioritisation can take various forms, such as cost or frequency of occurrence.

Pareto's Law (also known as the 80:20 rule) states that 20 per cent of causes give 80 per cent of the effect, eg, 20 per cent of customers generate 80 per cent of turnover. Whilst certainly not a rigid rule it is a useful guide.

A Pareto diagram is a bar chart that summarises items by their frequency and organise them in order of decreasing frequency. Each bar represents one category and the vertical axis shows the frequency or importance of occurrence. The total frequency for each item is shown by the height of its bar.

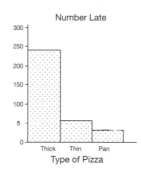

Benefits of Pareto diagrams

* Provide a graphic method for prioritising issues.
* Help to separate the vital few from the trivial many.
* Provide a means of viewing issues from different perspectives.
* Assist in monitoring effectiveness of improvement efforts over time.
* Can be used to compare the rank order of problems.

Pareto diagram construction

1. Decide on possible cause categories (use C & E diagram).
2. Collect the data.
3. Select appropriate scales.
4. Rank the cause categories.
5. Label the axes.
6. Plot the bars on the graph.
7. If 'others' is a significant category, consider breaking it down into specifics.

Scatter diagrams

A scatter diagram provides a picture of the relationship between two variables. It does not summarise data but investigates potential causes and other relationships. It may help demonstrate the strength of a relationship between two variables but cannot, however, serve as proof that a causal relationship exists. Only subject-matter knowledge can substantiate a causal relationship.

Benefits of scatter diagrams

- Depict a relationship between two variables.
- Explain what would otherwise appear to be random variation in the response variable, by taking the explanatory variable into account.
- Help identify variables that affect the variable of interest and are more controllable.

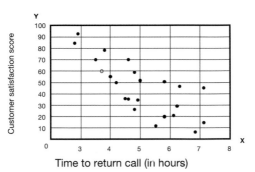

Time to return call (in hours)

Cause and effect relationships

An explanatory variable is one that influences, affects, or controls the other variable. The explanatory variable is often referred to as the independent variable.

A response variable depends upon or is influenced by the value of the explanatory variable. The response variable is often referred to as the dependent variable.

Theories about the two variables having a cause and effect relationship should be based on subject matter knowledge and not solely on a strong pattern in a scatter diagram: it can help to substantiate the theory or give reason for further investigation.

Theory of knowledge

Process managers need to understand the nature of learning (PDSA).
They must also be able to describe things so that others understand.
Such subjects have engaged great minds for centuries. This handbook
concentrates on aspects which are evidently and quickly useful at
work, but you will find it a rewarding field to study at length.

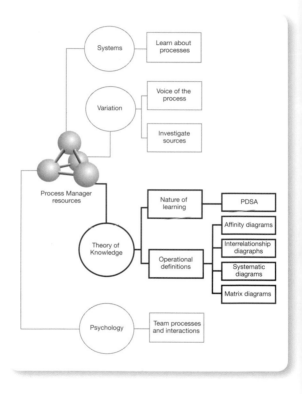

The PDSA cycle

A key to the theory of knowledge is Deming's PDSA cycle, a flowchart for thinking, learning and planning. Flowcharting in everyday processes can often demonstrate opportunities for learning. PDSA is also at the heart of the improvement team's processes described in section 4: structured problem-solving processes incorporating the planning of experiments which are critical to the learning organisation.

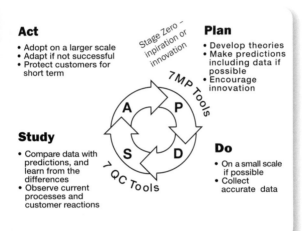

Act
- Adopt on a larger scale
- Adapt if not successful
- Protect customers for short term

Stage Zero – inspiration or innovation

7MP Tools

Plan
- Develop theories
- Make predictions including data if possible
- Encourage innovation

Study
- Compare data with predictions, and learn from the differences
- Observe current processes and customer reactions

7 QC Tools

Do
- On a small scale if possible
- Collect accurate data

Following the PDSA cycle results in learning or new knowledge, gained when outcomes do not agree with predictions. It is in fact the scientific method, making theories explicit and welcoming challenges to them. This is different from many people's idea of knowledge, which is more often an accumulation of information or data unrelated to theory and not useful for improvement.

You may not be able to choose where you enter the cycle, but if you can study first this will enable you to come up with some theories and make initial plans.

The PDSA cycle is a closed loop, effective for learning from data or experience from existing processes. However, projects, strategic management and innovation require breakthroughs in thinking and Deming proposed a Zero stage of the cycle. Some of the methods useful for it are summarised from page 3-5 onwards.

Operational definitions

These are a powerful concept which enable customers and suppliers to agree the measures which are to be met in order to achieve Customer Satisfaction.

These are called 'True Quality Characteristics'. These enable the supplier to defuse 'in process measures' which will result in the achievement of the True Quality Characteristics.

Developing operational definitions

Step 1: Determine the true quality characteristics required for satisfactory performance by capturing the voice of the customer.

- Meet face-to-face with the customer.
- Talk to the customer's employees who work directly with the product.
- Visit the customer to see the product/service in use.

Step 2: Determine the method of measurement. Sometimes the 'true' customer requirements (e.g. softness, comfort) cannot be measured directly so 'substitute' measures need to be found.

- Agree with the customer the specific measures that will become the substitutes.
- Evaluate the relationship between the substitute and true characteristics by experimentation, using PDSA.
- Ensure the customer understands the measure and the relationship.
- Determine the data collection method, including –
  - the sampling method;
  - material handling requirements; and
  - any requirements for retention of material for subsequent validation.
- Determine the steps in the measurement process, including –
  - the specification of any measuring equipment;
  - the set-up and use of the measuring equipment;
  - reference to any standards or specifications;
  - the recording method; and
  - the analysis and feedback methods.

Step 3: Develop acceptability criteria on the measure.

- Confirm that the criteria reflect your promise or guarantee to the customer.
- Ensure that the criteria do not limit improvement efforts.
- Reach agreement with the customer on the criteria.
- Define what needs to happen if the criteria are not met.
- Create a process continually to update the criteria.

> *"Without an operational definition, investigation of a problem will be costly and ineffective, almost certain to lead to endless bickering and controversy."*
>
> Dr. W. Edwards Deming

A planning model

The *Seven Management and Planning Tools* are intended for developing plans within multi-disciplined teams. Four of the seven are described here, two in the Processes section (arrow diagram on page 1-10 and PDPC, a contingency analysis tool, on page 1-14).
It is useful to relate their use, and that of other planning methods with which you may already be familiar, to a four phase planning model. This breaks the plan part of the PDSA cycle into logical subsets when considering a new project — (I) issue definition, (II) analysis of action, (III) organisation of action, and (IV) contingency.

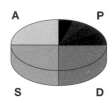

In separating an established set of tools, often taught as an integrated whole, we seek to broaden their use as we have found them to be useful in circumstances far beyond what may be thought of as project planning. They are management tools — the way things can be accomplished more effectively.

Planning phase I: defining the issue

What are we trying to accomplish? The first step in establishing a plan, or understanding a process, is collecting and organising information about the situation. This might be numerical data but is often verbal data, ideas, facts, guesses, or opinions. The organisation of this information will help people move from creative, amorphous thoughts to logical groupings (affinity diagram), and
from general subject headings to logical relationships (interrelationship diagraph).

Issue statement

Issue statements influence the whole planning process and must be carefully considered. They must be worded to help generate creative and diverse ideas. Beware of questions which require action responses. The team needs to have a common understanding and agreement of the wording of the issue statement and this may take some time.

Affinity diagram

The purpose of an affinity diagram is to enable team involvement in generating, organising and consolidating verbal information at the start of any project. This information is grouped into natural clusters that bring out the latent structure of the subject under study and promote creative solutions. Initial investigation of a process may require comprehensive exposure of the issues rather than creativity and the words of the issue statement need to convey this.

Example of a tidied up affinity diagram

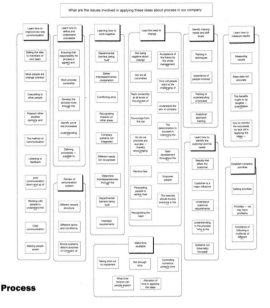

Process

1. Clearly define the issue statement so as to generate responses. Be careful not to limit yourself by the question. Everyone must agree on the question before proceeding. Statements often begin with phrases like:

   'Factors that influence...'

   'Elements of...'

   'What are the issues involved in... ?'

   'What would be the characteristics of success of... ?'

   'What makes... effective?'

   'What are the barriers/problems involved in... ?'

2. Use silent idea generation to collect the input. Each idea should be written on a Post-it™ or a 3x5 card in large letters. Respond with a considered thought rather than single words, but write only one idea per card. (If there is the word 'and', break it up on two or more cards.)

a. Each member writes all the ideas they can.

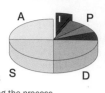

Definition

b. Place idea cards on a table or wall in random fashion. Clarify if needed, but don't discuss. Similar versions of the same ideas should be retained. Ideas may be added at any time during the process.

3. Cluster the ideas.

a. Spread out the ideas so that they can be seen and are within the reach of everyone.

b. In silence, team members group ideas they consider similar together. These clusters may be broken up and recombined at any time. If an idea seems to belong to two clusters, the card may need to be duplicated.

c. When no moves have taken place for a few minutes, ask if everyone is satisfied. If so, go to the next step. Some small clusters or individuals may not seem to fit with any of the other clusters.

4. Define the clusters.

a. The team next defines a header card for each cluster. Start with the most straightforward clusters. Approach the lone ideas last. Discuss what the central theme is for these ideas. The header card should capture the meaning, or the affinity, all of the cards in the cluster have for each other. The statement on the header card should be specific and consistent. One way to check the header card is to answer this question:

> 'If you take all the cards away, does the header card represent what this cluster means?'

If the team is unable to come up with a satisfactory header for a particular cluster, table the discussion and move to the next cluster. Then return to that cluster.

The headers need to be consistent with the original question. (If the question were 'What are the problems...?' then the headers should be stated as problems.)

b. In the discussion for defining the meaning of the cluster, the team may decide that a cluster should be broken up into two distinct clusters, or that some cards really belong with another cluster. Another possibility is to make subclusters within a main cluster.

If the clusters are reformed:
- start with the most straightforward; and
- work with the stragglers last.

c. If the ideas are on paper, a boundary may be drawn around each cluster.

Flowchart for an affinity diagram

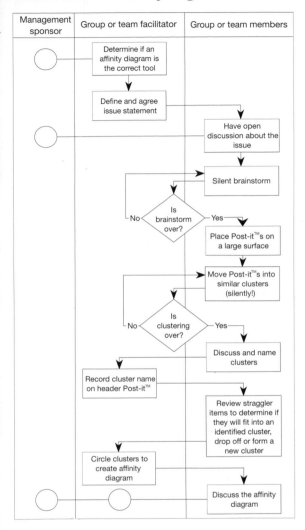

Management sponsor	Group or team facilitator	Group or team members

5. Take care of the stragglers. There are three possible actions:

   a. A card may belong in one of the defined clusters.

   b. An individual card may be dropped if everyone agrees it is not related to the issue statement.

   c. An idea may form a cluster on its own. Additional cards may be generated to go with it.

Process variations

1. Any unstructured idea-generating approach may be used, including:
    a. open brainstorming with responses written by a leader or recorder on a flipchart or Post-it™s simultaneously.
    b. open brainstorming with each person recording their own responses (no flipchart or recorder).

2. The idea cards may also come from the following:
    - Customer complaints or comments
    - General responses from in the workplace
    - Confidential employee survey (for example, responses to a question such as 'If you could change one thing...').

3. After idea generation, the team members might read out each idea as they place them on the wall. This helps clarification before clustering starts.

4. Identifying headers. Two variations include:
    a. briefly discussing the meaning of each idea (and how it fits with the others) before naming the cluster; and
    b. before discussing what the header card should be, each member decides on his/her own what the cluster means, then takes it in turn to suggest a name.

5. After initial silent idea generation, post and discuss all ideas. Then allow time for a second idea generation period (either at the same meeting or after everyone has had some time to reflect).

Tips for facilitators

1. If the team is not familiar with the process, explain it carefully and ask them to suspend judgement of it. See if they would be willing to take part first and discuss the pros and cons afterwards.

2. Spend some time defining and agreeing upon the issue for idea generation. It is important to get the best issue statement possible before starting.

3. Don't let people try to identify potential cluster headings before they begin to share their input about the issue statement.

4. If the team is comfortable with one particular style of brainstorming/idea generation, use it.

5. Encourage the idea generation to continue well beyond the initial 'off the top of the head' phase.

6. Maintain silence during the clustering phase. Be strict on this, and on non-verbal signals.

7. If an item is continually moved back and forth between clusters, it may be put on one side and discussed after the initial clusters are named. It may be that the idea has several meanings that can be broken down and combined appropriately with the named clusters.

8. Ground rules may need to be set if inappropriate behaviour starts during the clustering phase, for example items cannot be stuck out of the reach of other team members, items cannot be removed.

9. The number of clusters will vary depending on the issue and the team. Generally, the number of clusters is between six and twelve. If a team has more than 15 clusters, encourage them to continue a little longer.

10. Encourage participants to add ideas later as they get them – even after the clustering is completed.

11. Headings should be as specific as possible and still capture the meaning of the cluster. Broad headings, such as communication, customer, suppliers, are not acceptable.

12. Don't allow an individual to dominate any part of the process. Try to plan each step carefully to ensure everyone contributes. For example: a) when generating ideas, maintain silence and let individuals take turns to speak out and b) in defining cluster headings, have each person write down what they perceive the cluster to represent, then read each one before coming to a consensus on the header statement.

13. It is best not to work with too large a team. However, when working with more than twelve:
    a. Choose a large open room and allow plenty of time so team members can circulate freely.
    b. The team may be divided into two or more subteams to work on different aspects of the issue (eg, 'What do we need to implement...?' and 'What are the barriers to implementing...?'). Keep the affinity diagrams from the two teams separate. Do not combine results from two teams into one affinity diagram.
    c. Have the entire team go through the idea generation phase, but make a subteam of about six people do the clustering and header cards.
    d. Do not attempt to break up a large team into two subteams to go through the affinity process separately using the same issue statement, and then combine the results.

14. Do not use another team's affinity diagram to complete or use as input to the next tool, the interrelationship diagraph.

15. Header card test: 'If all the cards in the cluster are taken away, does the header card still convey the theme of the cluster if shown to someone new?'

16. The affinity process is creative and helps the team to see the issue from a new perspective. However, it can be seen as a way to build a new perspective, so be careful when rearranging the idea cards into clusters. Wholesale reordering sometimes unintentionally supports an old mindset.

17. While discussing a cluster, it may become evident that there are two or more themes in the cluster. These may form subclusters for the original cluster.

18. Make sure that the scope of the question is appropriate for where the team is in the process. All too often teams brainstorm before understanding the situation completely.

Interrelationship diagraph

The purpose of the ID (or relations diagram) is to identify and develop a consensus about logical and sequential connections (ie, cause and effect relationships) between components of a problem, issue or system. Input can come from an affinity diagram.

The process for producing an interrelationship diagraph is:

1. Generate an affinity diagram.
2. Place the issue statement at the top of a flipchart as a title.
3. Take the headers from the affinity diagram and arrange them in a circle below the issue statement.
4. Draw a line connecting ideas which are related. Use an arrow head at one end of the line to indicate the direction from cause to effect. Use only one-way arrows.
   Ask two questions:
   - 'Are these two ideas related?' If so, draw a line. The team must decide from the beginning whether they will draw a line for a weak relationship.
   - Determine the direction of the arrow by asking, 'Which idea has a greater effect on the other?'
   Go around the circle of ideas systematically so all pairs have been compared only once.

5. Once all relationships have been noted, count the number of arrows pointing away (OUT) and pointing towards each header (IN). Place these numbers on top of the idea card (ie, number OUT/number IN).

Interrelationship Diagraph

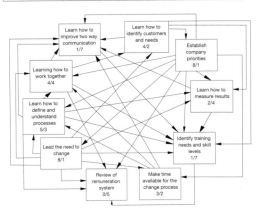

What are the issues involved in applying these ideas about process in our company?

6. Place each header card in approximate sequence with the number of arrows pointing away (OUT) on the y-axis and number of arrows pointing towards (IN) on the x-axis.

7. Identify the key cause factors, enablers or drivers. These are the header cards with the most arrows pointing away from them. Draw a heavy line around each of these cards.

8. Identify the key effect factors, outcomes, or receivers as the headers with the most arrows pointing towards them.

9. Use the final interrelationship diagram as an aid in planning the priorities of actions on the objectives. The priorities are the actions associated with the upstream drivers.

Example of a neatly drawn ID

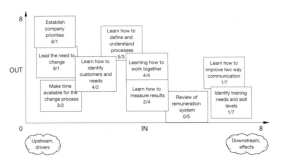

3-12

The next actions may be –

- general exploration of the priority objective(s), perhaps by another affinity/ID process; or
- a detailed breakdown of the parts of the objective to discover accountabilities or relationships, for which a systematic diagram may be useful.

Process variations

a. An interrelationship diagraph can be constructed from an affinity diagram using one header card and the cards listed under it. The team may want to brainstorm for more ideas to fill in any gaps about the problem. This may be useful if the need to begin working on one cluster is determined and more direction is needed as to how to begin.

b. An interrelationship diagraph can be constructed using all the cards from an affinity diagram. Although this method focuses the ID on all aspects of the problem, it can yield a cumbersome ID. (Only the strong relationships would be identified.)

c. A team can also use as inputs the most likely ideas of a cause and effect diagram, the categories of a Pareto diagram, or inter-departmental critical success factors.

d. Construct an interrelationship diagraph to understand any related set of ideas or criteria.

Tips for facilitators

1. Keep details of each cluster available to consult in case the meaning of a heading is unclear.

2. Ask the two questions in step 4 of the process in turn, for each pair of header cards.

3. Do not allow two-headed arrows.

4. In most cases the team should focus attention on the key causal factor, rather than the key effect which is often too far downstream in the process for the team to address directly.

5. Avoid making the decision on the key causal factor solely by the numbers. Ask whether the result makes sense and ensure the group has not overlooked any relationships.

6. Share the results with the sponsor of the team and/or with customers.

7. If the team reaches an impasse, skip the comparison and return to it later. (Mark the pair clearly to remember which one needs to be addressed again. A dotted line is useful for this purpose.)

Process for interrelationship diagraph

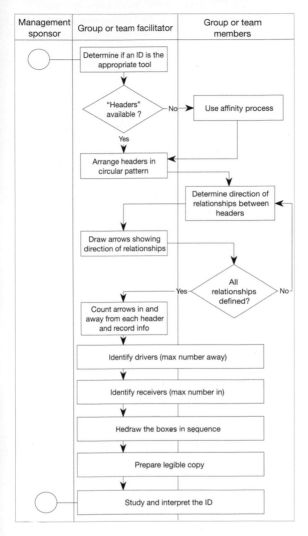

8. Do not rush the construction of an ID.

9. In estimating the amount of time needed to construct an ID, note that the number of one-to-one comparisons increases quickly with the number of header cards.

10. Let the team decide if they should use consensus or 2/3 majority to decide the direction of an arrow. In either case, encourage both sides to express their views fully before a decision is made.

11. A team will decide at the beginning of the process what strength of relationship merits a line. Once a team begins the process, it must not change this definition. (If a large number of comparisons are to be made, avoid lines for weak relationships so that the process moves more quickly.)

12. After the ID has been constructed, display the header cards from left to right – drivers to receivers.

13. Answer the questions in step 4 of the process according to the present situation, not as you would like it to be.

14. Often there is a hidden cycle in an ID. Some team members may not be comfortable with this. Remember that cycles often occur naturally. Try to understand how this is a reinforcing cycle/system and at what point the team may be able to intervene in the cycle to affect change. Peter Senge's book, *The Fifth Discipline*, has some useful insight into this and other behaviours of systems.

15. Occasionally a team analyses an ID where the direction of the arrow depends on whether the team is considering the current or the future/should-be situation. The decision must reflect the chosen situation. Do not mix current and future on one ID.

Planning phase II: analysing actions

The second step of establishing a plan or understanding a process: developing details of what is to be done.

Systematic diagram

Purpose

To determine the specific actions needed to accomplish an objective or the detail appropriate to ensure that everything has been considered in a process or project design. A systematic (or tree)

Systematic diagram

diagram can be used to determine the most effective means for solving a problem or accomplishing an objective. It breaks down the issue into the most specific level of detail needed to identify actionable items that will lead to problem resolution or objective accomplishment.

Process

1. The team should select an objective that all agree on. (ID)

2. Generate actions related to the objective. For example, ask 'What actions can we take to achieve ...?' or 'What must we do in order to...?' If the need for a tree diagram has developed out of an affinity and ID, then you should start by reviewing the ideas from the affinity cluster which the ID showed to be upstream.

3. Follow the affinity process to cluster the ideas from the previous step. The headers from these clusters will form the major branches of the tree. Try to break each cluster into sub-clusters (to form the smaller branches). Continue to subdivide the branches. Organise the diagram with the objective on the far left, the major headers in a column next to it ... with the most specific detail (action) cards in the right-most column. (Do not try to organise by time order.)

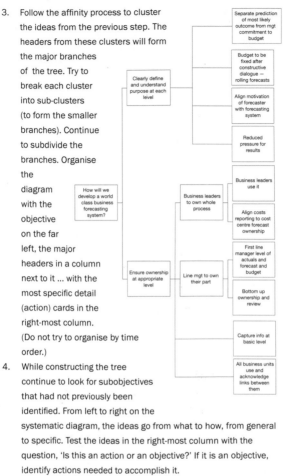

4. While constructing the tree continue to look for subobjectives that had not previously been identified. From left to right on the systematic diagram, the ideas go from what to how, from general to specific. Test the ideas in the right-most column with the question, 'Is this an action or an objective?' If it is an objective, identify actions needed to accomplish it.

5. Are there any additional actions or components of an action plan that need to be included?

6. Align the action items in a column on the far right, connecting the boxes with lines.

7. Once you have a complete list of potential action items, you may realise that not all items are possible. A small number may be needed to accomplish the objective. One of two approaches may be used to 'prune the tree'.

   a. Consider each major branch in its entirety. Ask, 'Is it necessary to include actions in this area to accomplish our objective?' If no, go to the next major branch. If yes, identify those actions and mark them.

   b. Check to see if any broad approaches are mutually exclusive before examining detailed action items.

   Since only one of these approaches would be taken, consider the risks, benefits, costs and time involved with each. It is helpful to

Process for systematic diagram

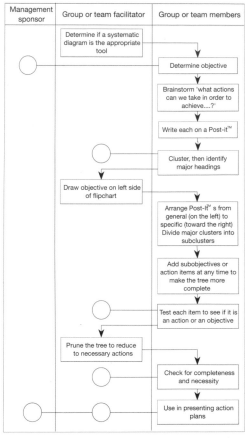

identify which actions are associated with each approach (eg, by colour coding) if they are scattered throughout the systematic diagram.

8. Final test. Now that there is a smaller list of action items, ask the following:

   • If these are accomplished successfully, will we achieve our objective?

   • Are any of them unnecessary?

   • Are they manageable — what are the resources and time required compared to what is available?

Keep in mind the following in producing a systematic diagram:

• Use a large work space (the position of the ideas doesn't have to be perfect).

• The last item in each row should line up and be an actionable item. Ask if it is an action or an objective.

- Remember that there is not necessarily any time sequence either from top to bottom or left to right.
- Be prepared to be frustrated at first – complex issues can have well hidden structures!

Systematic diagram

Process variations

a. After brainstorming in step 2, instead of using the affinity process, the team may discuss what the major branches should be. This may be preferable if there is considerable knowledge and experience within the team on the issues involved.

b. An individual (facilitator/leader) or subteam could bring to the team meeting possible ways to break down the objective into the major categories.

Tips for facilitators

1. Prepare the team for the amount of time needed to construct a systematic diagram. A number of one to two hour sessions or one to two days off-site is usually required, depending on the complexity of the issue.

2. Continue to brainstorm additional idea cards throughout the process. Removing gaps between objectives and actionable items is critical to this process.

3. Do not get stuck in sequential thinking. You may need to rearrange the idea cards several times to achieve the appropriate structure for the problem/objective under study.

4. Do not stop the process until the team has achieved a sufficient level of detail upon which they can take action.

5. The level of detail required in the action items will depend, in part, on the team constructing the diagram. For example, a quality steering team of executives might have an action item, 'Develop TQM overview course,' which is given to a training team or expert.

6. In considering the final list of action items, bear in mind how much support can be expected from those not on the team in carrying them out.

7. Do not use the systematic diagram if:
   - only a simple implementation is needed;
   - only a short amount of time is available;
   - a large team is involved (ideally not more than about four!);
   - there is not enough information available on the actions needed

Planning phase III: organisation of action

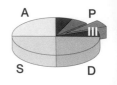

Once details of what to do are agreed, phase three of the planning model covers the hows. Matrix diagrams are valuable tools in assigning people or process to actions or in establishing priorities.

Matrix diagram

There are many applications for the matrix diagram including –

1. using the planning model as a responsibility matrix;
2. choosing among alternatives or in setting priorities;
3. relating customer needs to product, quality function deployment (QFD), or service characteristics, service quality deployment (SQD).

There are two types of simple matrices:

- The L matrix (a two-dimensional chart which helps to explain the interrelationships between two problems/variables using a column and row format);

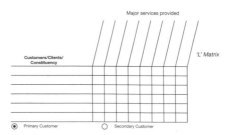

- The T matrix (a matrix that combines two 'L' matrices and is used to compare, correlate, or study two problems/variables with respect to a third problem/variable).

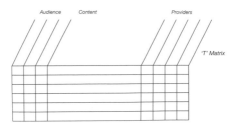

Process for matrix

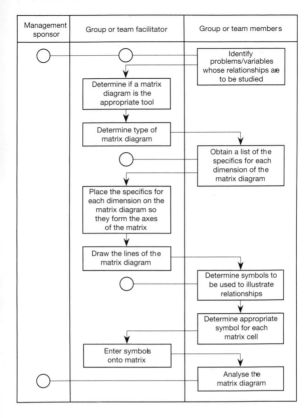

Matrix process

1. Use when a team needs to identify the relationships between two lists or variables, for example, between people and tasks.

2. Decide on the matrix format, for example L-shaped or T-shaped.

3. Place the items of the two lists or variables on the matrix diagram so they form the axes of the matrix. Items can be recorded directly onto a flipchart or placed on individual Post-it™ notes/cards.

4. Draw in the lines of the matrix.

5. Determine the symbols to be used to illustrate the strengths of relationships. Include a key to the symbols on the matrix diagram.

    a. The most common symbols used to depict functional responsibilities are:

        Primary responsibility

        ⊙ Secondary responsibility

        Ⓢ Should receive information.

    b. The most common symbols used to depict relationships

between quality characteristics are:

⊙ Extremely important

◯ Very important

△ Important.

6. For each row, discuss and agree the relationship between the row topic and each of the column topics.

Matrix

   a. If there is no relationship, leave the cell blank.

   b. If there is a relationship, agree its strength and enter the appropriate symbol in the cell.

7. Analyse the matrix by –

   a. studying and understanding the relationships between the variables being studied;

   b. balancing workloads;

   c. identifying and resolving any problems between the issues/ variables being studied.

Tips for facilitators

1. If possible, the team leader or facilitator should make up the matrix form and axes before the team meeting.

2. Obtain consensus on the specific items that are placed on each of the axes. Discuss each item to obtain common understanding before assigning symbols to illustrate relationships. While completing the matrix, you may discover that an additional row (or column) is needed.

3. Use symbols in the matrix that are most meaningful for the situation. An additional set of symbols to consider are the International Weather Symbols:

Symbol	Correlation	factor
Blank	No correlation	0
◗	Some correlation	3
◑	Moderate correlation	5
◕	Strong correlation	7
●	Very strong correlation	9

Define clearly what is meant by each symbol **before** assigning them to elements of the matrix. Include a key with the matrix.

4. Be sure the definition of the strength and nature of a relationship (ie, when to place a symbol at intersection) does not change in the course of constructing the matrix.

5. Interpretation: look at the number of symbols in each row and column. Too many or too few could be a problem. (Sharing primary responsibility may also be a problem.)

6. Use it as a means of communicating to people not on the team.

7. Do not put a person (position) on the matrix unless that person has agreed to the action or the action is in their job description.

Prioritisation matrix

Prioritisation matrices are used to help prioritise
items or to help choose between alternatives.

1. Determine weights for the criteria. Note: If the
   previous rating scale used larger scores for
   items with higher preference, then the weights for the criteria
   should be larger weights for the more important criteria. However,
   if the previous rating used lower scores for more preferable items,
   the criteria should have smaller weights for the more important
   criteria. (Or, you may prefer to just reverse the original rating
   scale.)

2. For each column (alternative), discuss and agree if the alternative
   meets the criteria.

   a. If the criteria is not met, leave the cell blank.

   b. If the criteria is met, agree its strength and enter the
      appropriate symbol in the cell.

3. For each column (alternative) multiply the rating for each strength
   (1, 3, 9) by the weight for that criteria and add up all weighted
   scores for that alternative.

4. Compare the totals for the alternatives (using, for example, a
   Pareto diagram).

5. Interpret. Determine if smaller or larger scores are
   most preferable. Do not automatically choose the largest/smallest
   score.

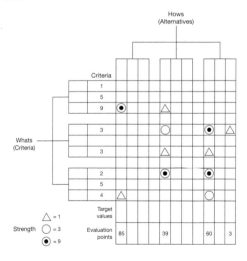

Psychology

Learning how to work together in reducing variation and optimising processes.

This is the hardest of all the aspects of the System of Profound Knowledge to summarise. The study of motivation, communication and interaction between people is critical in leading and enabling transformation. All the tools featured in this book are designed to facilitate learning, and are likely to challenge opinions of the way your organisation works. We recommend leaders review and consider their own and their team's behaviour and knowledge in at least the following fields.

*   Leading teams
*   Facilitating teams and meetings
*   Coaching individuals and groups
*   Presentations and training
*   Understanding intrinsic and extrinsic motivation
*   Stress and time management

We feature some issues which are particularly relevant to those leading process improvement and innovation.

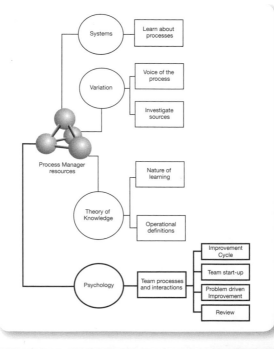

System and process customers

All processes should be aligned to their customers – direct or indirect, in the system or beyond. A logical approach to understanding and improving processes, will help to uncover customer needs and wants but may still fail to generate delight.

Dr Kano's model helps the psychology of understanding customers by –

- segmenting aspects of customer needs and wants in order to identify latent delight factors;
- realising that things asked for are taken for granted;
- encouraging innovation to be ahead of customer expectations; and
- standing in the shoes of customers, in order to identify the expected factors, gains respect and tolerance.

Three Categories of Customer Requirements

After Kano's model of customer satisfaction as a function of need fulfilment

- Since 1982, Dr. Noriaki Kano has been Professor, Department of Industrial Management Sciences and Engineering, Science University of Tokyo.

All these aspects of listening to process customers apply just as much to internal relationships as to paying customers.

Bear this picture in mind whilst working to improve the system or to fix problems as they occur.

The Improvement Cycle

The Improvement Cycle is a systematic, data driven approach to business and quality improvement and is based on the PDSA cycle. It is summarised on the next three pages.

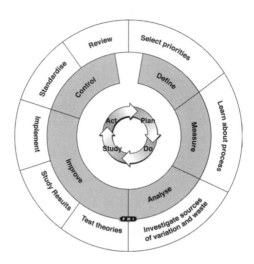

Using the Improvement Cycle

The Improvement Cycle relates closely to the Six Sigma DMAIC model (Define, Measure, Analyse, Improve, Control).

General points
- Record each step in the process as it happens.
- Review each step before moving on to the next.
- Make notes against each subsection.
- Provide sufficient information to assist review and to enable future reference.
- Recruit someone from outside the team to ask:
  - Do the words demonstrate that the team fully understands the charter?
  - Has the team maintained a 'process' focus?
  - Is the team membership appropriate to the process?

Improvement Cycle	Project Task
Select Priorities	Select strategic issue to address
	Charter team
	Form the team
	Define SIPOC / System map
	Verify performance with data
	Agree the contract
	Define the review process
Learn About the Process	Flowchart process
	Steamline and standardise
	Agree customer requirement
	Select key measures
	Define data collection
	Listen to the voice of the process
Investigate Sources of Variation and Waste	Brainstorm and prioritise root causes
	Collect data to verify causes
	Select root causes to address

Improvement Cycle	Project Task
Test Theories	Define possible solutions
	Select solutions to test
	Develop a plan for the tests
	Carry out the tests
Study Results	Study the results of the tests
	Define next steps to take
Implement	Understand implementation environment
	Determine competency
	Develop implementation plan
	Develop communication plan
	Monitor plan
	Review
Standardise	Deploy standardised improvements
	Monitor process and react appropriately
Review	Review conclusions and lessons learned
	Define generic learning fan-out
	Define future plans

Effective Teams

"A team is a small number of people with complementary skills who are committed to a common purpose, performance goals, and approach for which they hold themselves mutually accountable."

The Wisdom of Teams, Katzenbach and Smith

Whenever teams work on an improvement project the work going on in the team process operates at three levels simultaneously. The three levels are the task, the task process and the socio-emotional process.

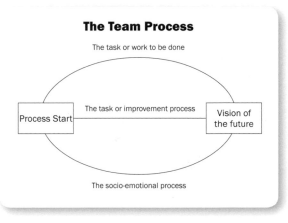

The Team Process

The task or work to be done

Process Start — The task or improvement process — Vision of the future

The socio-emotional process

The task level is the work to be delivered.

The task process level is how the improvement process will be approached.

The socio-emotional level is the feelings and relationships the team bring with them and develop as the work progresses.

It is the mismatch between all three levels that create difficulties for the team and lead to reduced effectiveness. Effective teams are aware of all three levels and can integrate working at level three whilst working at the the other two levels.

For improvement teams to be successful the leaders of an organisation first need to:

- Ensure the vision is clear.
- Identify the Critical Success Factor (CSF).
- Determine the actions/processes that achieve the CSFs.
- Identify high priority processes.
- Charter the improvement team.
- Support the improvement efforts.

Projects selected should be:

Meaningful
–   Linked to organisational objectives and goals.
Manageable
–   Not too complex and have a reasonable timescale.
Measurable
–   Data already exists and additionals can be created.

Process for forming a team

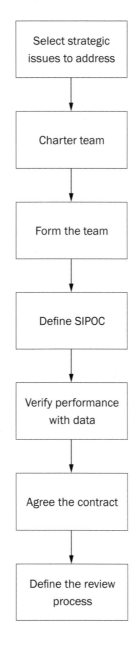

Select strategic issues to address

↓

Charter team

↓

Form the team

↓

Define SIPOC

↓

Verify performance with data

↓

Agree the contract

↓

Define the review process

Chartering the team

To start the process of gaining a common understanding, teams should be provided with a team charter. This will set out the following:

Purpose
-     Why are we doing this.
Business Case
-     What will this achieve.
Team
-     Who is to be involved.
Scope
-     Which areas, processes.
Enablers
-     What needs to be in place (budgets, resources etc).
Barriers
-     What might hinder the process.
Resources needs
-     What support is needed, other resources.

This document will be less specific than the team needs, and the team will use it to compile a contract!

Developing effective team contracts

Teams experience most difficulties when their contract is woolly, unclear or unrealistic either in scope or timescale. Directives to improve the accounts payable process, reduce arrears to customers, scrap or inventory, or fix the problem on IMA28 (a tea-bagging machine) are simply not helpful enough to focus a team's efforts.

A good team contract should address four issues and be agreed by the primary stakeholders:

A. The business case or reason for being
* Why does the team exist?

B. The project objectives that include:
* The process under consideration
* A process measure
* Discussed direction
* Target to be reached
* Timescale for completion

C. The scope/boundaries of the effort
* Who will be impacted and/or involved?
* Where (process boundries?)
* Design and other change constraints

D. The expected project milestones
* What are the key activites and the target dates for the various activities?

E. Players
* Who will be involved in the project?
* What will be everyone's responsibility?

F. Resource estimate
* What people, capital and expense money are likely to be needed?
* Who is funding the budget?

Steps for clarifying and agreeing the team contract

1. Review purpose for team communicated in team charter document. Discuss why this is important for the business.

2. Identify what each team member believes is the reason for the team's existence.

3. Discuss team member commitment to team's reason for existence.

4. Develop a draft team contract which communicates the team's primary purpose, the scope of the project, milestones and desired outcomes as understood by team members.

5. Discuss, revise and agree team contract with primary stakeholders (sponsors, customers, suppliers).

6. Negotiate with managers to agree –
   - expectations;
   - responsibilites;
   - review protocols; and
   - how the manger will remove barriers.

Illustration of a well formed contract

Project purpose
   - Improve the percentage of on time payments from 40% to 95%.

Business case
- For the past years, on average, the process has only paid 40% of invoices on time.

Successful completion will –
- give the company £30k/yr prompt payment discounts;
- eliminate double payments for re-submitted invoices (currently 5%).

On time payment of invoices is critical to cash flow.

Key players
   - Champion John Jones
   - Team leader Colin Shaw
   - All members of the department (6)

Scope
- Our department
   - receipt of invoice to request for cheques

- No major I.T. spend

Milestones

Milestone	Duration	Estimated finish
Flowchart current process	6 hrs	March 31
Simplify process	4 hrs	April 5
Identify & analyse causes for delay	8 hrs	April 14
Select & test countermeasures	48 hrs	May 31
Implement & confirm results	32 hrs	June 30
Standardise improvements introduce monitor sytem	48 hrs	July 31

Enablers

- Time to carry out work
- Training team in improvement techniques

Barriers

- Inadequate measures
- Concerns about identifying peoples mistakes

Support Estimate

- 6 people, 4hrs/wk for 6 months   £10,000
- Travel   £1,000
- Sundry   £2,000
  Total   £13,000

Forming the team

Effective teams will possess the following components:-

1. Purpose and Priority
   - Task must warrent a team and priority to the organisation
2. Capabilities
   - Skills, knowledge and experience to achieve the goal
3. Roles and Responsibilites
   - Each member has a role and feels accountable for the success of the team
4. Operating Processes
   - The way in which the team will and ground rules generate and behave
5. Mutually agreed outcomes
   - All can see the relevance of the project to the organisation's goals
6. Leadership
   - An attribute demonstrated by all members of the team

Select the right team

Who should be on the team? Consider the following:

1. At the work level, people who:
   - do the work;
   - know the process best.
2. At the supervisory level, people who are:
   - the direct management of the process;
   - responsible for the improvement of the subprocesses.
3. At the management level, people who are:
   - the owners of the process;
   - responsible for overall process improvement.
4. Customers who:
   - receive the output of the process;
   - can help explain the nature of the problem.
5. Suppliers who:
   - provide inputs to the process;
   - are often part of the solution to the problem.
6. Technical experts who have:
   - studied/worked in the process;
   - specialised knowledge about the process.

Determine the mode of Operation

Definition of the team's mode of operation

The team's mode of operation is a combination of its roles, responsibilities, operating processes and ground rules. By making these explicit the team gains clarity about the way it is going to work together to achieve its purpose.

Refering to the team process model, which has 3 elements
1. Task level (The content of the work)
2. Task Process level (How the work gets done)
3. Socio-emotional level (How team members relate to each other)

The team, to be effective, should exhibit the following behaviours at each of these levels.

Task level behaviours
1. Initiating
   - new ideas and suggestions
2. Information giving
   - clarifying facts, opinions based on knowledge and experience
3. Evaluating
   - help access quality of suggestions
4. Summarising
   - pull together ideas, offering conclusions

Task Process level behaviours
1. Planning
   - setting goals, outcomes and milestones
2. Structuring
   - define the steps to achieve purpose
3. Co-ordinating
   - combining activities of others
4. Assessing
   - Progress against planned outcomes and milestones

Socio-emotional level behaviours

1. Encouraging
   * supporting, sharing warmth
2. Harmonising
   * alleviating tension, valuing difference, using humour developmentally
3. Gatekeeping
   * ensuring everyone has chance to air ideas and feelings
4. Following
   * progress against planned outcomes and milestones
5. Observing
   * monitoring progress, providing feedback

Ground Rules

Setting ground rules allows the team to formulate expectations to guide the **administrative** and **behavioural** functions of the team's operation.

* Administration ground rules describe how the team will work together – organisation, meeting mechanics, etc.
* Behavioural ground rules make explicit the desired and agreed upon norms of behaviour.

The following administration questions will help your team come up with ground rules for working together.

Roles
* How will the team leader be selected?
* Will team leadership rotate? Monthly? Never?
* Who will keep time? How will proceedings be recorded?
* How will a facilitator be selected? Or, how will the team take care of facilitation needs?

Decision-making
* Who will be responsible for the agenda?
* Who will record the meeting minutes? Who should receive a copy of the minutes?
* What kind of decision-making process should our team use? Possible choices: autocratic, expert, autocratic with input from the team, majority rule, concensus, unanimous consent.

Logistics
* How often do we want to meet?
* How long will our meetings be?
* When do we want to meet?
* Where do we want to meet?

Behavioural

What behaviours do we consider important in the healthy functioning of the team?

Consider issue such as:
- Punctuality
- Preparedness
- Confidentiality
- Listening
- Contribution rates
- Modes of speech
- Handling disagreement and criticism
- Handling dysfunction
- Work allocation

Effective team meetings

Role	Responsibilities for effective teams

Leader:
- Before the meeting should:
    - Plan the meeting place and time.
    - Set the agenda.
    - Invite team members and others as needed.
- During the meeting should:
    - Keep the team on track.
    - Involve everyone.
- After the meeting should:
    - Follow up decisions and action items.
    - Begin to plan for the next meeting.

Recorder:
- Minute important information, decisions, and action items.
- Send out minutes and action register.

Members:
- Come prepared.
- Participate.
- Take on action items.

Facilitator:
- Support the leader in managing team process.
- Act as a navigator; do not lead.
- Give guidance in the use of methods.
- Do **not** do the work for the team.

Technical Adviser:
- Provide expertise as needed.

Sponsor:
- Act as communication link between team and a management steering team or local steering team.
- Advocate for team.

Consultant:
- Provide initial training and direction.
- Work with leader and facilitator to develop their abilities.
- May attend team meetings if needed.

Follow a process improvement strategy

- Seek improvement through attention to assignable causes for all routine processes. (This is Kaizen as properly defined.)
- Use PMI's problem driven improvement approach for problems as they occur, when they are thought to be relatively high priority and require immediate response.

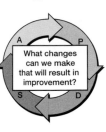

What changes can we make that will result in improvement?

- Use PMI's Improvement Cycle for issues with a broader scope probably requiring cross-functional co-operation.

Whatever the route it is vital, once the objectives and measures have been established, to make the PDSA cycle turn as rapidly as possible. This alone will produce learning and the results that everyone is looking for.

Evaluate team processes

At the end of each meeting:

1. Ask each person to state a word or phrase that best describes their impression of the meeting.
2. Ask each person to comment on how well the meeting went for them.
3. Use a flipchart to record:
   - what went well;
   - where improvement is needed;
   - actions to improve future meetings.
4. Evaluate the meeting using the team's ground rules as a benchmark.
5. Obtain written feedback from team members.

Decision-making strategies

The following chart describes the types of decision-making strategies, their definitions, and the pros and cons of each strategy*. While consensus decision-making may be the preferred strategy, it might not always be the appropriate one.

Strategy	Definition	Pros	Cons
Autocratic	One person makes decisions for the entire team	It's quick. Responsibility is clear.	No support solicited. No feedback on decision
Expert	The person who knows the most about the topic makes the decision.	No team research needed. Responsibility is clear.	No feedback. No customer information included.
Autocratic with input from the team	A single person makes decisions but only after asking for the opinions of others involved.	It's quick. Some customer feedback is received. Responsibility is clear.	Frustration due to lack of follow-up.
Majority Rule	The decision is made by selecting a solution that is satisfactory to at least 50% of the team.	Democratic. It's quick.	Some members still lose. Responsibility unclear.
Consensus	All members consent to a decision; full consent means that members are willing to support the decision.	All members give feedback. All members support decision.	May take time.
Unanimous Consent	Everyone agrees and is completely satisfied with the decision.	All members agree.	May never happen.

* Developed by Marilyn Monda and Lori Silverman.

Consensus decision-making

Almost all the tools in this handbook are best used in team situations. Effective planning and implementation relies heavily on consensus decision-making. The task is to come to a decision which is supported afterwards by everyone – a decision is only as useful as its implementation, not its announcement at the time.

Definition of consensus

All team members consent to the decision; full consent means that members are willing to support the decision. Consensus does not require that all team members agree that the decision is the best that could be made, but that they will support it. This may not be easy and a process for getting there is very useful.

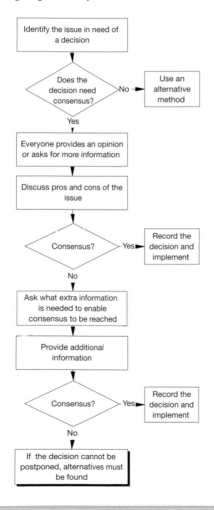

Proper use of many of the tools can help teams come to a consensus by illustrating, defining, and communicating the issue, problem, or process the team is studying.

Process

1. Determine if a decision needs consensus. (Consider how soon the decision must be made, amount of support, buy-in needed, importance of decision.)
2. All members provide input and/or request more information.
3. Discuss alternatives – identify pros and cons; determine if the team has enough data to make a decision.
4. Determine if consensus exists.
5. If consensus does not exist, identify points of conflict and agreement. Seek creative alternatives and ways to meet major concerns.
6. Determine if decision needs to be made immediately.
7. If a decision does not need to be made immediately, decide if additional research, thought time, expert advice or data is necessary.
8. Gather additional input from sources identified in step 7.
9. Record the decision when a consensus is reached.

Problem-driven improvement process

This is a simple process designed to be driven rapidly in response to issues as they arise. It is supported by a PMI work book and facilitator guide. The next two pages summarise the key steps.

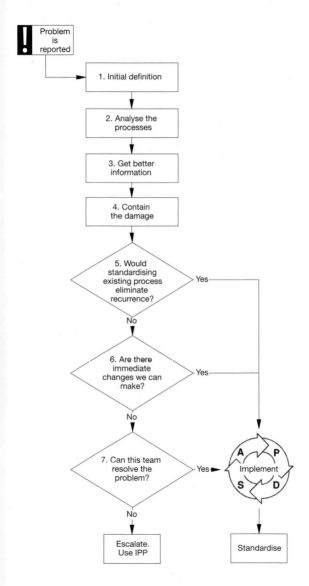

1. Initial definition

1.1 Define the problem as reported to the team.

1.2 Define the team members.

1.3 Describe the events and symptoms of the problem.

1.4 Retain any 'failures'.

1.5 Refer to appropriate database.

2. Analyse the process

2.1 Define the steps/operations to be studied.

2.2 List other parts generated by this process.

2.3 Redefine the team based on the scope of the problem.

3. Get better information

3.1 Further define the problem by:

- stating what is wrong;
- defining the difference between good and bad outcomes;
- asking 'Is it measurable? Can we identify the good from the bad?';
- identifying the pain that the problem is causing.

3.2 Collect data from both process and results measures.

3.3 Decide if the problem was a surprise, ie, was it an assignable (special) cause, or a problem that occurs on a regular basis?

4. Contain the damage

4.1 Identify implications for the customer.

4.2 Identify and implement any actions necessary to protect the customer.

4.3 Can we reclaim/rework any materials/goods?

5. Validate the process

5.1 Understand the process and ascertain that it was followed.

5.2 Check equipment and inputs.

5.3 If the process is followed, does it satisfy customer needs?

- Understand customer requirements.
- Check clarity of documented procedures.
- Check capability index.

6. Make any immediate changes

6.1 List ideas generated so far.

6.2 Brainstorm 'Other sources of variation in this process'.

6.3 Evaluate options for action.

6.4 Select one or a few options.

6.5 Conduct a contingency analysis.

7. Decide whether the current team can solve this problem.

7.1 Implement solutions and standardise if 'yes'. Update database.

7.2 Escalate to the next level of authority and/or form a broader team.

Reviewing the team's progress

The reviewer's preparation

As the reviewer, ensure you are clear about the many purposes of the review, and help the team to address all of them.

Reviews should:

- Discuss problems.
- Revise project plans if necessary.
- Celebrate progress.
- Transfer learning.
- Enable chartering managers to:
  - Keep the project focused and on track.
  - Ensure that the appropriate strategy is being followed.
  - Offer support to the team.
  - Remove barriers.
  - Encourage learning.
- Enable the team to:
  - Update managers on progress made.
  - Ask for help in dealing with barriers.
  - Work through difficult issues with managers.

The emphasis in these meetings should be on creating a learning environment and developing trust.

Use the phases of the Improvement Cycle as the structure of the reviews – each component of each stage can be regarded as a deliverable to be addressed before moving to the next stage.

Responsibilities after the project

After a project is completed, the chartering managers are responsible for ensuring that the changes made by the team are communicated and implemented so that they become part of daily work, ie, ensure standardisation occurs. They should also review any systemic issues and barriers that arose during the project and address them to increase the success of future projects.

Use the following questions as a guide.

- To what extent did the team use data to back up their claims?
- To what extent did the team systematically use the chosen improvement methods?
- How adequately did the team address fundamental issues?
- What difficulties did the team experience in generating data?
- What was attendance at meetings like?

Note: The role of the chartering managers is not complete until the changes are introduced, improvements accomplished and maintained, and standardisation has been implemented.

Glossary of terms/Index

Page references in square brackets [ ], section number in bold, are to the subjects covered within this handbook.

Affinity diagram [**3**-6] A powerful method of organising and categorising brainstormed ideas at the start of projects. One of the Seven Management Tools.

Aim (noun) See Vision. What we are trying to create. Leadership of change is required to achieve it. It must be shared by all to be of any value.

Aim (verb) What we do – 'We aim to provide...'. Used in this context it relates to the **mission** or **purpose**. It need not imply change from the present state. Much confusion arises when people do not distinguish between the different kinds of aim.

Analytic data [**2**-3] Data gathered from within processes, used for prediction and improvement.

ANOVA (Analysis of Variance) A significance test that partitions variation into its component parts and can be used to compare two or more sample means.

Assignable cause variation [**2**-12] Causes of variation that arise due to special circumstances, fleeting events or change of process and which can frequently be traced to a single source.

Autonomation Designing processes, machines or production lines that stop when an abnormality occurs.

Benchmarking The process of comparing processes against others from competing or 'best-in-class' organisations.

Black Belt Helps any team in the application of Six Sigma and other process improvement methods. A typical Black Belt will have successfully completed an appropriate training course and at least a significant project, and passed the certification process.

Business process re-engineering Another way to describe innovation or radical redesign of processes, which may be ingredients of any transformation. Requires the skills of process improvement for effective achievement.

Capability [**2**-22] Process capability studies compare the variation of a process with the specification. Capable processes are essential for **Lean manufacturing**.

Cause and effect diagram [**2**-25] Used in conjunction with **brainstorming**, it shows the relation between a problem, quality characteristic or condition (effect) and the factors (causes) that produce it. One of the **7QC Tools**.
Also referred to as the *Ishikawa* or fishbone diagram. Effective for analysing fairly concrete problems, it works less well with cultural and organisational issues. (See **affinity diagram**, **interrelationship diagraph**.)

A

Champion Acts on the organisation's behalf to maximise the chances of success for a programme or project. They will usually be a member of the senior team managing the wider system within which improvement work is expected to proceed.

Chi-square test A significance test used to check the independence of data in a contingency table.

Common cause variation [**2**-12] A cause of variation that is inherent to the way the process is organised and operated.

Consensus A decision-making strategy where all members consent to the decision and agree to support it.

Continuous flow A contrived state where a number of sequential processes are balanced, allowing material or information to pass through them one piece at a time, without delay. This is regarded as the most efficient way of repeatedly producing a specific product or service.

Control chart [**2**-13] A graphic representation of values that represent the behaviour of the process — the basis for discriminating between **common and assignable causes** of variation. Also known as a process behaviour chart, it is used to assess the capability of a process and for prediction of its on-going performance. One of the **7QC tools**.

Control limit [**2**-16] A boundary on a control chart, defining the range of **common cause** process behaviour — a 'voice of the process'; not to be confused with specification limit which represents the 'voice of the customer' (or boss!).

Customer [**1**-9] User of a product or service of the generating process. May be inside or outside the organisation. The next process is considered the customer for a process within a system. Customers need to be seen as the reason for existence of processes, not just as recipients of the output.

Cycle time The amount of time taken by those elements of work that actually transform the product or service in a way that the customer is willing to pay for.

Data collection [**2**-2] The process of gathering information to be used as a basis for future decisions. A check sheet should be formulated for data collection purposes and the reasons for collection should be an inherent part of its design.

Design of experiments A discipline for planning and analysing experiments where multiple, possibly interacting, adjustments can be made.

DFSS **D**esign **f**or **S**ix **S**igma: utilises the current most powerful tools and methods for designing/redesigning a new product and/or service for a commercial market. DFSS improves quality of introduction, reduces life cycle costs, addresses service and support issues.

DMAIC [**4**-3] 5-step improvement model widely used in Six

Sigma programmes. The steps are: **D**efine the project goals and customer (internal or external) deliverables. **M**easure the process to determine current performance. **A**nalyse and determine the root cause(s) of defects. **I**mprove the process by eliminating defects. **C**ontrol future performance.

Enumerative data [2-3] Data used to report the results of processes, often for management judgement and reward rather than for prediction and improvement. cf. *Analytic data*.

Facilitation A process that an individual uses to aid a team in reaching its full potential, through identifying and eliminating obstacles, and effectively guiding the team in the accomplishment of its mission.

Failure modes and effects analysis A methodology for understanding the critical elements of a system and designing processes to eliminate the chance of failure.

Flowchart [**1**-4] A diagram or map of a process which uses symbols (for actions, yes/no decisions and other events) in a linear sequence to show what actually happens in a process or in designing new processes.

Gantt Helps organise the various activities involved in a project into manageable groups of tasks. Sometimes referred to as a "milestone" chart. It is a horizontal bar chart that graphically displays the time relationships between the different tasks in a project. Can be used to refine the schedule, compare different strategies, and make the plan as efficient as possible.

Green Belt May be the leader of an improvement team. As a participant they help their natural work group apply improvement methods effectively so that they can improve the way work gets done. The level of competence to be attained by all managers and supervisors.

Histogram [**2**-7] A graphic tool for displaying the shape of a distribution of values.

Hypothesis testing A hypothesis test is a process in which you assume an initial claim to be true and then test this claim using sample data. Hypothesis tests include two hypotheses: null hypothesis (H_0) and alternative hypothesis (H_1).

Idea Generation [**2**-26] Used to elicit ideas from all group members. There are many ways of generating ideas and careful consideration of people and circumstances is needed before selecting the method.

Impact wheel Useful tool for assessing the risk of a potential action. The risk assessment component of an implementation plan contains a team's assessment of what could go wrong if actions are implemented.

Improvement Cycle [4-3] The PMI 8-step, systematic, data driven approach to business and quality improvement, which is based on the PDSA cycle. The steps are: **S**elect priorities – define the most important problems for the business and set-up appropriately supported teams. **L**earn about the process – understand how the process is operated and performing at present. **I**nvestigate sources of variation – explore what is causing the unacceptable performance at present. **T**est theories – test possible solutions to the root causes of the problem. **S**tudy results – ensure solutions will provide robust solutions to the required level of performance. **I**mplement – carefully plan all aspects of the full scale implementation, both hard and soft. **S**tandardise – understand how the improvement will be locked in place and monitored to ensure future consistent performance. **R**eview – understand and fan-out both specific and generic learning about the project and review.

Improvement teams Teams comprising colleagues from within a function, or across functions, that work through an improvement process to achieve their objectives.

Interrelationship diagraph [**3**-11] A method of establishing causal or time sequences between sub elements of a major issue. One of the **Seven Management Tools**. It is more effective with complex and sensitive subjects than the **cause and effect** diagram. Also known as a **Relations diagram**.

Input A resource introduced into a system or expended in its operation which helps to attain a result or output.

Kaizen Japanese term meaning continual improvement. Also used by some to denote Lean manufacturing workshops.

Knowledge [**3**-2] The learning which results from comparing the predictions made in the Plan stage of the **PDSA cycle** with data collected in the Do stage.

Lead time The time taken by one piece (part, product or service transaction) to move all the way through a number of linked processes or a complete value stream, from start to finish. This will include non-processing time such as waiting.

Lean manufacturing The application of business improvement and standardisation to enhance quality, cost and delivery.

Loss function A concept developed by Taguchi to demonstrate that variation from target causes continually escalating costs. Understanding the loss function encourages progressive reduction of variation rather than mere compliance with specification.

Master Black Belt Individual developed beyond Black Belt level to advise, support and possibly manage Black Belts.

Matrix diagram [**3**-19] Method of relating two or more collections of characteristics to enable, for example, the prioritising of improvement or development efforts. One of the key tools of **QFD**. One of the **Seven Management Tools**.

Metric An indicator of results of a process, attributes of a product or service.

Operational definition [**3**-3] A three-part description of what an organisation or group believes its customers want or need and how they will measure if it is achieving this aim. The components are: 1. true quality characteristics (or 'voice of the customer'), 2. substitute characteristics (or 'voice of the process'), which includes methods of measure, and 3. criteria for success – the actual number to be aimed at.

Output The result produced by a system or process. It may be a product or a service.

Pareto principle [**2**-27] Popularised by Juran, it categorises the causes of a condition into the 'vital' few and the 'trivial' many. Displays the 80/20 principle, and can be shown by a diagram.

PDPC [**1**-14] Process decision programme chart. A simple contingency analysis tool, one of the **Seven Management Tools**.

PDSA cycle [**3**-2] **P**lan, **D**o, **S**tudy, **A**ct. Commonly referred to as the Deming cycle. It provides an iterative, learning approach to process improvement. Also known as PDCA.

Poka-yoke The Japanese term for mistake proofing. It is a series of techniques employed to prevent mistakes being made, or failing that, detecting them at source.

Policy deployment Involves identification, communication, contribution, understanding and buy-in from all employees with respect to the organisation's *vision*, *mission*, principles, long-term goals, plans and values. Also referred to by the Japanese term Hoshin Kanri.

Process [**1**-2] Set of interrelated activities which transform a set of inputs into one or more outputs. They are hard to distinguish from a system, but might usefully be seen as components of a system.

Process boundaries Limits of the process decided upon for definition or team work. They are often arbitrary and will change over time.

Process control The act of achieving and maintaining a stable process. Stability is not a natural state for any process.

Process improvement (PI) A continual endeavour to learn about causes and effects in a process in order to reduce complexity and variation. It is accomplished by identifying and removing **assignable causes** and then by process redesign to reduce **common cause** variation.

Process Improvement Team (PIT) A team working on a process or problem within it related to increasing customer satisfaction, efficiency or effectiveness. A PI team consists of people who work in the process day to day and their customers, suppliers and supervisors.

Process Management (PM) A methodology that aims to optimise the organisation as a system, determining which processes need improvement and/or control, setting priorities, and providing leadership to initiate and sustain process improvement efforts.

Process owner Responsible for the entire process – communicating its aim, optimising the performance in the context of the whole system, and leading efforts to improve it. A role carried out on behalf of and with the consent of affected colleagues.

Profound Knowledge, Deming's System of A powerful model for leadership, learning and change.

Programme management The collection of disciplines for planning, staffing, implementation and review of a change programme.

Pull system A control loop, where a customer process sends production signals upstream to its supplying process, thus ensuring it produces only what is needed, when it is needed. A pull system may have many loops, linking processes backwards from the point of actual customer demand, creating a chain reaction of production. May be physical or electronic.

Quality Indefinable! One definition of quality is: a reliable, consistent product or service that meets or exceeds customers' requirements at a price they are willing to pay. Another universal definition is 'on target with minimum variation'.

Quality Function Deployment (QFD) The term for a collection of disciplines, founded in deep understanding of customer needs and wants, used to speed the development of major projects and new products. Based upon many hierarchical *matrices*.

Regression Analysis Method of modelling the relationship between one or more independent variables and a dependent variable.

Run chart [**2**-6] A time-sequence graph of individual values. One of the **7QC tools**.

Scatter diagram [**2**-28] A graphical technique used to assess the relationship between two variables. One of the **7QC tools**.

Seven QC tools Form the everyday backbone of any quality improvement effort. The 7QC tools are useful in the plan stage and in checking the effectiveness of the countermeasures set into motion in the Do stage of the PDSA cycle (see PDSA cycle). The 7QC tools are: data collection sheets, run charts, histograms, control charts, cause and effect diagrams, Pareto diagrams and scatter diagrams.

Seven Management and Planning Tools Developed during the early 1970s in Japan. Designed to enable managers to structure the evolution of a project, from concept through to implementation. The 7MPs are: affinity diagram, interrelationship diagraph, tree (systematic diagram), prioritisation matrix, matrix, arrow diagram and process decision programme chart.

SIPOC [**1**-17] A single page summary containing a high level view of: the process, customers & suppliers, measures, current performance and theories on sources of variation.

Six Sigma improvement teams Multi-disciplined, cross-functional or cross-company teams that work on specific process improvement, innovation, policy or technological change projects. They have a life span based on the completion of their purpose.

They are chartered (i.e., started) by a steering team or by management, supported by a Black Belt and sponsored by their Champion.

Six Sigma philosophy Used both as a philosophy and a goal of performance. The philosophy is a structured approach to continuous business improvement. The goal is a measure of performance of a process defined as defects per million opportunities.

Special causes of variation See **assignable cause**.

Stable process [**2**-12] A process that is predictable because it is subject to variation arising only from common causes. The property of being in statistical control. (Rare!)

Statistical process control (SPC) A method by which a process is studied and variation is reduced over time. The resulting data are analysed to identify **assignable causes** of variation. People with knowledge of the process work to identify and reduce recurrence of assignable causes and to understand and reduce **common cause** variation.

Stratification Used to gain more information about the process through the use of the other tools. Stratification takes a set of measurements and places each measurement into one of two or more categories that may give some insight to sources of variability. So, instead of a single data set, there are several smaller sets that can be displayed and compared.

Steering team Comprises leader, members and facilitator. Main responsibilities are: managing the process improvement efforts; assessing requirements for and overseeing the training and education within their area of responsibility; communicating progress to all interested parties; and leading by example.

Supplier A person or organisation that provides goods or services for use by the process being studied.

System Represents organisations as they really are and includes customers, suppliers and the flow of materials and information. The major system components are: the 'Gemba' – parts of the system which add value to inputs in the customers' interest; support processes – enable the Gemba to operate; and change processes – take feedback from customers and environment to develop policies and lead major changes to the Gemba.

Takt time 'Lean' concept which defines the frequency at which one part should be produced to meet customer requirements. The 'heartbeat' of the process.

Tampering Adjusting a **stable process** without knowledge of whether the cause of the problem is **assignable** or **common**.

Total productive maintenance (TPM) A company-wide system aimed at maximising effective output at minimum total life-cycle cost. Essential to **Lean manufacturing**.

Total Quality Management (TQM) An unsatisfactory phrase, widely misused. TQM is a management system or philosophy which emphasises people, process management, customer service and the elimination of waste and rework.

TRIZ A problem solving method, developed by the Russian G Altshuller and colleagues, that accelerates a project team's ability to solve problems. TRIZ is the acronym in Russian for 'Theory of Inventive Problem Solving'. Now it is an international science of creativity that relies on the study of the patterns of problems and solutions, not on the spontaneous creativity of individuals or groups.

t-Test Significance test used to compare one or two sample means.

Unstable process [**2**-12] A process that is subject to variation arising from **assignable** as well as **common** causes.

Variation Quantitative change in value between cases or over time caused by common and/or assignable causes.

Vision statement An expression of what success looks like for the organisation. The goal is to produce a mental image to strive toward — aligning the organisation to produce 'creative tension' between current reality and the vision. To be of any value it must be shared by all in the organisation, and this takes a lot of patience in its development. The **mission** or **purpose** is the way in which progress is to be made.

References

There are thousands of business books and a whole range of histories, biographies and novels which offer insight into people as individuals and groups. Anything to do with leadership and change is relevant to our topic.

To view current papers published by PMI visit the publications section of www.pmi.co.uk